THE
BEHAVIOR OF LAW

THE
BEHAVIOR OF LAW

Donald Black

Department of Sociology
Yale University
New Haven, Connecticut

Academic Press
San Diego New York Boston
London Sydney Tokyo Toronto

The quotes on pages 35 and 36 cited to Goffman (1956) are from "The Nature of Deference and Demeanor," by Erving Goffman. Reproduced by permission of the American
Anthropological Association from the *American Anthropologist*, 58:481, 490, respectively
1956.

The quotes on pages 107–108 cited to Nader and Metzger (1963) are from "Conflict
Resolution in Two Mexican Communities," by Laura Nader and Duane Metzger. Reproduced by permission of The American Anthropological Association from the *American Anthropologist*, 65:589, 591, respectively, 1963.

The quotes on pages 57 and 120 cited to Selby (1974) are from *Zapotec Deviance: The
Convergence of Folk and Modern Sociology*, by Henry A. Selby. Copyright 1974 by
The University of Texas Press and reproduced by permission.

The quotes on pages 34 and 77 cited to Suttles (1968) are from *The Social Order of the
Slum*, by Gerald D. Suttles. Copyright 1968 by The University of Chicago Press and reproduced by permission.

Find Us on the Web!   http: //www.apnet.com

Academic Press
A Division of Harcourt Brace & Company
525 B Street, Suite 1900, San Diego, California 92101-4495

United Kingdom Edition published by
ACADEMIC PRESS   (LONDON) LTD.
24/28 Oval Road, London NW1

Library of Congress Cataloging in Publication Data

Black, Donald J.
    The behavior of law.

    Bibliography: p.
        1.   Sociological jurisprudence.   2.   Deviant
behavior.   I.   Title.
Law   340.1'15   76-23297
ISBN 0–12–102650–7 (cloth)   ISBN 0–12–102652–3 (paper)

Printed in the United States of America
98 99 IBT 12 11 10

Contents

6

Social Control   105

7

Anarchy   123

Preface

This book contains a number of propositions about the variation of law across social space. The purpose of these propositions is to predict and explain this variation, and so to contribute to a scientific theory of law. Theory of this kind has practical applications, and also applications to the study of other social life.

The propositions address a wide range of legal variation, including, for example, variation in what is defined as illegal, who calls the police or brings a lawsuit, who wins in court, who appeals or wins a reversal, who is handled by what procedure, and—across time and place—how much law, if any, appears in social life. By implication, these propositions also predict and explain many facts usually addressed by theories of deviant behavior, and, reformulated, they predict and explain other kinds of social control. Finally, by implication they specify the conditions for anarchy—social life without law—and, applied to existing trends, they forecast the future of law.

It may be assumed that theory of this kind is valuable for its own sake, and in the following pages no effort is made to justify this work on other grounds. Nevertheless, the contents of this book may be of interest to those who would act upon the world. For instance, with these propositions it is possible to calculate legal risks and advantages from one case to another, to engineer a legal outcome in or out of the courtroom, to reform a legal system, or even to design a community with little or no law at all. But this book does not judge the variation of law, nor does it recommend policy of any kind. Rather, it is merely an effort to understand law as a natural phenomenon.

The formulations in this book also illustrate a theoretical strategy with applications beyond the study of law. The strategy assumes that social life is a subject matter in its own right, apart from individuals as such. It assumes that a science of this subject matter should be—like older sciences—quantitative, predictive, and general in scope. It incorporates earlier theoretical traditions to some degree, but includes other elements as well, such as its own imagery, concepts, and framework of analysis. Accordingly, it might be said that the theory of law is an example, and not the ultimate concern of this work.

Acknowledgments

Over a period of years, I have received financial and other support from several research and training programs: the Russell Sage Program in Law and Social Science and the Law and Modernization Program, both of Yale Law School, and the Program in Deviant Behavior, Social Control, and Law of the Department of Sociology, Yale University. In addition, a committee of Yale College awarded me a Junior Faculty Fellowship for the academic year 1973–1974, allowing me to devote all of my time to this book. I am grateful to the people who made this support possible.

For reading and commenting upon the manuscript, I thank M. P. Baumgartner, Maureen Mileski, Laura Nader, and Guy E. Swanson. M. P. Baumgartner helped with every draft I wrote, and made other contributions too numerous to acknowledge.

I also thank Mary Markiza for typing the manuscript, and I thank the people at Academic Press for their commitment and craftsmanship.

1

INTRODUCTION

Behavior is the variable aspect of reality. Everything behaves, living or not, whether molecules, organisms, planets, or personalities. This applies to social life as well, to families, organizations, and cities, to friendship, conversation, government, and revolution. Social life behaves. It is possible to speak of the behavior of art or ideas, the behavior of music, literature, medicine, or science.

* * *

Social life has several variable aspects, including stratification, morphology, culture, organization, and social control. Stratification is the vertical aspect of social life, or any uneven distribution of the conditions of existence, such as food, access to land or water, and money. Morphology is the horizontal aspect, or the distribution of people in relation to each other, including their division of labor, integration, and intimacy. Culture is the symbolic aspect, such as religion, decoration, and folklore. Organization is the corporate aspect, or the capacity for collective action. Finally, social control is the normative aspect of social life, or the definition of deviant behavior and the response to it, such as prohibitions, accusations, punishment, and compensation.

Every aspect of social life has many expressions, then, and all of these vary as well, increasing and decreasing from one time and place to another. It is possible to formulate propositions that predict the quantity of each from one setting to another, and to explain the behavior of each accordingly (see Braithwaite, 1953; Hempel, 1965). Every aspect of social life may even be used as a strategy of explanation: Stratification thus explains social life of other kinds (e.g., Tocqueville, 1840; Marx and Engels, 1888; Bendix and Lipset, 1953), and the same applies to morphology (e.g., Durkheim, 1893; Parsons, 1966; Bott, 1971) and to culture (e.g., Weber, 1904–1905; Sorokin, 1937; Merton, 1938b), organization (e.g., Michels, 1911; Swanson, 1971; Smith, 1974), and social control (e.g., Ross, 1901; Etzioni, 1961; Goffman, 1963). Moreover, each of these strategies is independent of the others, and it is possible to apply all of them, at once, to the behavior of social life of every kind. Consider, for example, the behavior of law.

LAW

Law is governmental social control (Black, 1972:1096; see also Radcliffe-Brown, 1933; Pound, 1939:3–9; Redfield, 1964). It is, in other words, the normative life of a state and its citizens, such as legislation, litigation, and adjudication. By contrast, it does not include social control in the everyday life of a government service, such as a post office or fire department, since this is the social control of employees, not of citizens as such. Nor does it include discipline in a government school, prison, or in the military, since this is not the social control of citizens—as such—either. By this definition, then, law is only one kind of social control. Furthermore, in this sense, many societies have been anarchic, that is, without law (see pages 123–124; compare Malinowski, 1926:15; Hoebel, 1940:45–48; 1954:18–28; Pospisil, 1958:257–278). In this sense, in fact, much social life in every society is anarchic.

*   *   *

Law is a quantitative variable. It increases and decreases, and one setting has more than another. It is possible to measure the quantity of law in many ways. A complaint to a legal official, for example, is more law than no complaint, whether it is a call to the police, a visit to a regulatory agency, or a lawsuit. Each is an increase in the quantity of law. So is the recognition of a complaint, whether this is simply an official record, an investigation, or a preliminary hearing of some kind. In criminal matters, an arrest is more law than no arrest, and so is a search or an interrogation. An indictment is more law than none, as is a prosecution, and a serious charge is more than a minor charge. Any initiation, invocation, or application of law increases its quantity, even when someone brings law against himself, as in a voluntary surrender, confession, or plea of guilty. Detention before trial is more law than release, a bail bond more than none, and a higher bail bond more than one that is lower. A trial or other hearing is itself an increase of law, and some outcomes are more law than others: A decision in behalf of the plaintiff is more law than a decision in behalf of the defendant, and conviction is more than acquittal. The more compensation awarded, the more law. And the same applies to the severity of punishment as defined in each setting: the greater a fine, the longer a prison term, the more pain, mutilation, humiliation, or deprivation inflicted, the more law. A court order or command of any kind, by any legal official, is more law as well. A pardon, commutation, or parole is less law, but a revocation of parole is more. If a government provides treatment for a deviant, such as hospitalization or rehabilitation, this is also more law. The same applies to mediation or arbitration of a dispute. If a decision is against the plaintiff and he appeals, this is more law, and a reversal in his behalf is more as well. But if a defendant wins a reversal, this is less law. More generally, the quantity of law is known by the number and scope of prohibitions, obligations, and other standards to which people are subject, and by the rate of legislation, litigation, and adjudication. As a quantitative variable, law is all of this and more.

The quantity of law varies in time and space. It varies across the centuries, decades and years, months and days, even the hours of a day. It varies across societies, regions, communities, neighborhoods, families, and relationships of every kind. It varies with who complains about whom, who the legal official is, and who the other parties are. It varies with the ranks of these people, their integration into social life, their intimacy with each other, their conventionality, memberships, and reputations. It varies with every aspect of its social environment—vertical, horizontal, cultural, organizational, or normative. It varies across the world and its history, the settings of a society or community, the cases in a court, the daily round of a policeman. All of this is the behavior of law, and it is possible to explain all of it.

*   *   *

In addition to the quantity of law in general, it is possible to explain the style of law. This, too, is a quantitative variable. Several styles of law may be observed, each corresponding to a style of social control found more widely in social life. These are the penal, compensatory, therapeutic, and conciliatory styles of social control. Each has its own way of defining deviant behavior, and each responds in its own way. Each has its own language and logic (compare Gibbs, 1963; Nader, 1969:86–91).

In its pure form, penal control prohibits certain conduct, and it enforces its prohibitions with punishment. In case of violation, the group as a whole takes the initiative against an alleged offender, the question being his guilt or innocence. In compensatory control, by contrast, the initiative is taken by a victim. He alleges that someone is his debtor, with an unfulfilled obligation. He demands payment. Both penal and compensatory control are accusatory styles of social control. Both have contestants, a complainant and a defendant, a winner and a loser. For both, it is all or nothing—punishment or nothing, payment or nothing. By contrast, therapeutic and conciliatory control are remedial styles, methods of social repair and maintenance, assistance for people in trouble (compare Goffman, 1971: Chapter 4). It is not a question of winning or losing, all or nothing. Rather, in these styles of social control the question is what is necessary to ameliorate a bad situation. Thus, the goal of therapy is normality. In the pure case, the deviant himself takes the initiative in his own behalf. He is a victim and needs help. He seeks the services of a helper of some kind, and together they work to improve his condition. Finally, in conciliation, the ideal is social harmony. In the pure case, the parties to a dispute initiate a meeting and seek to restore their relationship to its former condition. They may include a mediator or other third party in their discussion, together working out a compromise or other mutually acceptable resolution. A summary of these four styles appears below:

FOUR STYLES OF SOCIAL CONTROL

	Penal	Compensatory	Therapeutic	Conciliatory
Standard	prohibition	obligation	normality	harmony
Problem	guilt	debt	need	conflict
Initiation				
of case	group	victim	deviant	disputants
Identity				
of deviant	offender	debtor	victim	disputant
Solution	punishment	payment	help	resolution

In reality, social control may deviate from these styles in their pure form, combining one with another in various ways. For example, a penal case may arise at the initiative of a complainant, acting for himself, as in compensatory control. Or a therapeutic case may have penal elements, as, for instance, when a group or a helper takes the initiative, while the deviant protests that he is normal and needs no help. Even with such combinations, however, most of the elements of each style cluster together, and in most cases it is possible to identify the dominant style. In any event, even where a single style does not dominate a case, it is possible to identify the elements in combination.

Like the quantity of law in general, the style of law varies across time and space. It varies across the world and over the centuries, and from one society or community to another. It varies across relationships, from one legal setting to another, from court to court, and from case to case. It varies with the stratification of social life, its morphology, culture, organization, and social control. One setting has more punishment than another, or more compensation, therapy, or conciliation. One person is punished, while another must pay for his damage; one is sent to a mental hospital, while another talks the matter over and finds a way to make peace. One is condemned, another incurs a debt; one is given sympathy, while for another life goes on as before. And, just as it is possible to explain the quantity of law in general, it is possible to explain the quantity of each of these styles. Both are aspects of the behavior of law.

THE THEORY OF LAW

It is possible to formulate propositions that explain the quantity and style of law in every setting. Each of these propositions states a relationship between law and another aspect of social life—stratification, morphology, culture, organization, or social control. Each explains the behavior of law across time and space, in all societies for all time, wherever it is possible to measure law and other aspects of social life. Each explains known facts about law and implies countless other predictions as well. Given trends in the evolution of social life, each even forecasts the future of law.

Consider, as an example, this proposition: *Law varies inversely with other social control* (see page 107). Note only its form and content, ignoring for now the known facts that it explains and the earlier theories that it implies (see pages 107–111).

Law itself is social control, but many other kinds of social control also appear in social life, in families, friendships, neighborhoods, villages, tribes, occupations, organizations, and groups of all kinds. Thus, the proposition states that the quantity of law increases as the quantity of social control of these other kinds decreases, and vice versa. So formulated, it applies wherever and whenever it is possible to measure the quantity of each. It applies to everything from the evolution of social life across the world to an encounter between two people on the street.

For instance, it predicts, all else constant, more law in societies where other social control is comparatively weak, and this applies to the history of a single society as well as across societies at a single point in time. It also applies across communities and institutions within a society. And the same proposition predicts that parties to a dispute are more likely to go to law if they have no other means of settlement. It predicts that a policeman is more likely to arrest an offender who is subject to no other authority. It predicts that a citizen is more likely to call the police if he has no one else to help him.

Consider only the relationship between law and social control in the family. The proposition that law varies inversely with other social control predicts, all else constant, more family law in societies with comparatively weak domestic authority. It predicts more juvenile law in societies with comparatively weak parental authority. At the same time, it predicts that a family with less social control of its own is more likely to call upon law to settle its affairs. It predicts that a woman without a husband at home is more likely than other women to call the police about her son. In turn, the police are more likely to arrest a boy who lives with just his mother than a boy who lives with both parents, and, later, they are less likely to release him. If he goes to court, a judge is more likely to order a severe sentence—or extensive treatment—for him than for a boy with more social control at home. On the other hand, the same proposition explains why, in general, juvenile law is less severe than adult law, since, in general, juveniles are subject to more social control of other kinds. In short, this one proposition has countless implications, and all are subject to a test of the facts. But the theory of law has other propositions as well. Other aspects of social life also predict and explain the behavior of law.

* * *

Theory of this kind predicts and explains social life without regard to the individual as such (compare Winch, 1958; Homans, 1964; 1967: Chapter 3). It neither assumes nor implies that he is, for instance, rational, goal directed, pleasure seeking, or pain avoiding. It has no concept of human nature. It has nothing to do with how an individual experiences reality. It has nothing to say about the responsibility of an individual for his own conduct or about its causes. Theory of this kind, then, has nothing to do with the psychology of law (compare, e.g., Schwartz, 1954). It is not at odds with psychological assumptions or theories, however, but is simply a different kind of explanation, a different way to predict the facts.

Consider arrest. It is possible to understand an arrest as a decision of the policeman, a psychological event. As such, it may be explained with variables such as the policeman's attitudes and perceptions, his background and training, the expectations of his supervisors and colleagues, and the actions and reactions of citizens, including those subject to his authority. It is possible, therefore, to have a psychological theory of arrest. But it is also possible to understand an arrest as law, a social phenomenon. It is an increase of law in social life, and, as such, it is understandable with the same principles that explain other kinds of law in other settings. It is possible, for instance, to explain arrest with the proposition that law varies inversely with other social control (see Black, 1971:1097, 1107–1108). Hence, a proposition that pertains to legislation, litigation, and adjudication, even to the evolution of law over the centuries, also explains why a policeman makes an arrest in one encounter and not another. But it does not explain the behavior of the policeman as an individual. It explains the behavior of law.

Not only does theory of this kind say nothing about the individual as such, it also says nothing about social life that is beyond a test of the facts. It does not assume or imply, for instance, that everything in social life has a function, or that a social system tends toward harmony or stability (compare, e.g., Radcliffe-Brown, 1935). It does not assume or imply that conflict or coercion or change inheres in social life (compare, e.g., Dahrendorf, 1959:157–165; 1968b). Thus, the proposition that law varies inversely with other social control does not assume or imply that social life has the social control that it needs, that law appears when other social control is ineffective (compare Firth, 1951:73; Schwartz, 1954), or that it equilibrates social life (compare, e.g., Parsons, 1962:59–60). And this proposition does not assume or imply that society ultimately benefits from law or that any particular segment of society ultimately benefits (compare, e.g., Chambliss and Seidman, 1971). It does not assume or imply anything about the purpose, value, or impact of law. It says only that the quantity of law varies with the quantity of other social control, and how. It explains the behavior of law, and that is all.

DEVIANT BEHAVIOR

Deviant behavior is conduct that is subject to social control (see Lemert, 1948; 1951; Erikson, 1962; Becker, 1963: Chapter 1). In other words, social control defines what is deviant. And the more social control to which it is subject, the more deviant the conduct is. In this sense, the seriousness of deviant behavior is defined by the quantity of social control to which it is subject. The quantity of social control also defines the rate of deviant behavior (see Kitsuse and Cicourel, 1963; Black, 1970). The style of social control even defines the style of deviant behavior—whether it is an offense to be punished, a debt to be paid, a condition in need of treatment, or a dispute in need of resolution. In short, deviant behavior is an aspect of social control.

Accordingly, illegal behavior is an aspect of law. Therefore, the theory of law predicts illegal behavior. It thus predicts the same facts as the theory of crime, juvenile delinquency, or other illegal behavior. Each predicts who is subject to law, but each has a different explanation. The theory of law explains illegal behavior with the same principles that explain law itself. The theory of illegal behavior, however, explains these facts with the principles that motivate an individual to violate the law, to become, for instance, a criminal or a juvenile delinquent. For example, one theory explains this motivation with deprivation, such as poverty or a lack of opportunity (e.g., Cloward and Ohlin, 1960); another with marginality, such as a lack of family or friends (e.g., Hirschi, 1969); another with participation in a subculture (e.g., Miller, 1958); and still another with the consequences of labeling a deviant as such (e.g., Lemert, 1967). Whatever the details may be, each explains illegal behavior with the motivation of the individual.

The theory of law predicts the same facts, but as an aspect of the behavior of law, not of the motivation of the individual. For example, the proposition that law varies inversely with other social control predicts crime and other illegal behavior at the same time as it predicts the quantity of law. It predicts the definition of crime; it predicts the crime rate itself. According to this proposition, for instance, an individual without social control at home is more likely to become a criminal—since crime is defined by law and law increases as other social control decreases. Thus, it implies that a child from a broken home is more likely to become a juvenile delinquent, since the conduct of such a child is more likely to be defined as delinquent (see page 7). The theory of juvenile delinquency predicts the same facts, but for different reasons (e.g., Thrasher, 1927:65, 339–342; Reiss, 1951; see also Cicourel, 1968: Chapter 2). Like the theory of law, moreover, the theory of every kind of social control predicts deviant behavior. Deviant behavior is, by definition, an aspect of the behavior of social control.

THE BEHAVIOR OF SOCIAL CONTROL

It is possible to formulate propositions that explain each kind of social control. Etiquette, for instance, or witch hunting, ethics and other social control in science, discipline in an organization, or psychotherapy—each of these varies in quantity and style. Each behaves. And the aspects of social life that explain one also explain another. Indeed, the theory of law suggests propositions that explain other kinds of social control as well. It suggests, in other words, aspects of the theory of social control.

2

STRATIFICATION

Stratification is the vertical aspect of social life (see Sorokin, 1927: Chapter 1). It is any uneven distribution of the material conditions of existence, such as food and shelter, and the means by which these are produced, such as land, raw materials, tools, domestic animals, and slaves. It also includes any uneven distribution of other property, even of luxuries and surpluses, insofar as these may ultimately be exchanged for the conditions of existence. Hence, it includes an uneven distribution of a currency of exchange, whether livestock, grain, shells, or money. In a broad sense, then, stratification is inequality of wealth (see Fried, 1960; 1967: Chapter 5; Kelley, 1976; compare, e.g., Parsons, 1940; Dahrendorf, 1968b).

Stratification itself has several variable aspects. One is the magnitude of a difference in wealth, or vertical distance. Another is the degree to which wealth is distributed into layers, each separate from the next, rather than a continuum (see Fallers, 1973: Chapter 1). This is vertical segmentation. The number of these layers is also variable, as is the size of one in relation to another. And the mechanisms of distribution vary, in some cases depending upon what people do, such as their work or other responsibilities, in other cases depending upon how and when they were born, their age, sex, race, place of birth, or lineage (see Linton, 1936:115–116). The movement of people from one rank to another, or vertical mobility, varies as well (see Sorokin, 1927: Chapter 7). In these respects and others, stratification varies across space and time, across societies and the settings of a single society, among individuals and groups, within and between families, organizations, tribes, and nations.

Stratification explains other social life. The theory of historical materialism, for example, explains diverse phenomena—such as religion, marriage, politics, and revolution—with the distribution of the means of production (e.g., Engels, 1884; Marx and Engels, 1888). The degree of inequality in general also explains many kinds of behavior (see, e.g., Tocqueville, 1840), as do other variable aspects of stratification. For instance, the location of people in vertical space explains how they vote (e.g., Lipset, 1960), why they revolt (e.g., Gurr, 1970), their psychiatric care (e.g., Myers and Schaffer, 1954; Hollingshead and Redlich, 1958), friendships (e.g., Curtis, 1963; Laumann, 1966:63–70), and intellectual life (e.g., Mannheim, 1927; Merton, 1968).

Stratification also explains law, its quantity as well as its style. It has long been recognized, for example, that wealthier people have a legal advantage:

> The universal spirit of Laws, in all countries, is to favor the strong in opposition to the weak, and to assist those who have possessions against those who have none. This inconveniency is inevitable, and without exception [Rousseau, 1762a: 200; see also Rousseau, 1762b:68].

Similarly, according to the theory of historical materialism, the owners of the means of production have this advantage (see, e.g., Engels, 1888:234–237; 1890:403–405). A number of other formulations also make claims of this kind (e.g., Rusche and Kirchheimer, 1939; Chambliss and Seidman, 1971; Quinney, 1974). Moreover, the quantity of stratification itself explains the behavior of law, and so does the location of law in vertical space, whether higher or lower, and its direction, whether downward or upward. First consider the quantity of stratification itself.

THE QUANTITY OF STRATIFICATION

For these purposes, the quantity of stratification is the vertical distance between the people of a social setting. This is measured by the difference in wealth, on the average, between each person or group and every other (see Paglin, 1975), and also by the difference between the lowest and the highest among them, or the height of the distribution (see Sorokin, 1927: Chapter 4). Accordingly, as long as the standard is the same—whether cattle, bushels of grain, or dollars—it is possible to compare the quantity of stratification across space and time. Variation of this kind predicts and explains the quantity of law:

Law varies directly with stratification.

Thus, the more stratification a society has, the more law it has. At one extreme are bands and simple tribes, such as the Eskimos and Plains Indians of North America, the Jibaros of Equador and Peru, the Ifugao of the Philippines, the Nuer of the Sudan, and the Tiv of Nigeria. Before contact with Europeans, these societies had little or no stratification across families (see Service, 1971: Chapters 3–4). Furthermore, they had little or no law.

With stratification across families comes the chiefdom, the simplest society with law of a permanent kind:

> A chiefdom differs radically from a tribe or band not only in economic and political organization but in the matter of social rank—bands and tribes are egalitarian, chiefdoms are profoundly inegalitarian . . . . The basic ordering of society . . . is hierarchical. The society is composed of individuals, families, kin groups or villages, and lineages which are unlike each other [Service, 1971:140, 148; see also Fortes and Evans-Pritchard, 1940:9].

Examples include the Northwest Coast Indians of North America, most Polynesian and Micronesian societies, the steppe nomads of Asia, assorted agricultural societies of Africa, and the Germanic and Celtic tribes of Europe, including, until recent times, the Highlanders of Scotland (Service, 1971: Chapter 5). In societies of this kind, the chief himself is law, and so it is his authority that varies directly with stratification. The quantity of stratification varied considerably across Polynesia, for example, and so, correspondingly, did the authority of the chief in each society (see generally Sahlins, 1958; see also Goldman, 1955). At one extreme were Pukapuka, Ontong Java, and Tokelau, with little inequality of wealth and little or no chiefly authority, social control being administered largely by families and elders. Somewhat more stratified were the Marquesas, Tikopia, and Futuna, and in these settings the jurisdiction of the chief was a bit wider, though punishment for disobedience was nearly always mild. Yet more stratified were Mangareva, Easter Island, Mangaia, and Uvea, and in these the chief had yet more authority. He occasionally levied severe punishments, for instance, but the penalty of death was rare. Finally, at the other extreme, were Hawaii, Tonga, Samoa, and the Society Islands, with the greatest differences in wealth found in Polynesia, and in these societies the authority of the chief was the greatest. Only in these did the chief directly exercise supervision over the daily life of households, for example, and he frequently inflicted severe punishments, such as destruction of the offender's property, banishment, and death (Sahlins, 1958: Chapters 2–5). The same principle explains why, in general, the Polynesian societies had more law than other Oceanian societies, such as those of New Guinea and Australia (see Sahlins, 1963).

The same principle explains the growth of the state (see Engels, 1884: Chapter 9; Fried, 1960; 1967). It explains, for example, the emergence and growth of the state in early Mesopotamia and Mesoamerica (Adams, 1966: Chapters 3–4; see also Adams, 1972:62) and in the Indus and Yellow River valleys, Egypt, and Inca Peru:

> If the term "class" is used to describe objectively differentiated degrees of access to the means of production . . . , the early states characteristically were class societies . . . . The restructuring of stratified clans along class lines has a vital but indirect relation to the growth of the state [Adams, 1966:79, 120; see also Fried, 1967: Chapter 6].

The same pattern appeared in Europe (see, e.g., Rusche and Kirchheimer, 1939), and it continues in the modernization of Africa, Asia, Oceania, and Latin America. As traditional modes of production and distribution disappear, inequality proliferates across the world and law increases in every way. Legislation increases, as do policing and inspection, litigation, damages, and punishment. People become more litigious. All of this applies across the regions and communities of a single society as well. In modernizing societies, for example, law comes first to the towns and cities, last and least to the bush, where tradition is still strong and wealth more evenly distributed. And, for that matter, the same applies across settings of every kind, even within a single community. There is less law among neighbors, colleagues, friends—less wherever people are more equal.

If they have a dispute, people of different ranks are more likely to take their problem to a court or other legal agency. In the rural villages of Turkey, for instance, nearly every dispute handled by a policeman or other official involves people of different ranks, whereas equals settle their problems by themselves (Starr, 1974:29–30). The same pattern is found in every society. Even case by case, then, law varies directly with stratification (but see pages 21–28 of this chapter). In criminal cases, for example, arrest varies directly with stratification between the offender and victim, as does prosecution, conviction, and punishment. In civil cases, the same applies to a lawsuit, a decision in behalf of the plaintiff, or compensation. In an accident between people of different ranks, for instance, a lawsuit is more likely and the judge is more likely to award damages to the plaintiff. Unequal neighbors are more likely to litigate their boundary dispute. A husband and wife with origins in different social classes are more likely to take their marital dispute to court, and the judge is more likely to grant a divorce. For that matter, if the members of a family have an uneven distribution of wealth among themselves, they are more likely to resort to law for problems of all kinds. The stratification of a family or other relationship may also vary over time, and, as this happens, the quantity of law may vary accordingly. Thus, a dispute that smolders for months or years between equals may suddenly erupt in a lawsuit with a change in the fortunes of one of the parties, such as an inheritance or profitable marriage (see Starr, 1974:36).

Just as stratification varies between one citizen and another, so it does between a citizen and a legal official, such as a policeman, prosecutor, or judge. Law increases with the stratification of this relationship as well (but see page 23). This applies to the relationship between an official and a defendant, victim, plaintiff, or witness— whoever has a role in the case. And it applies to the relationship between each party and the members of a jury: The more stratified the relationship, the more law the jury is likely to apply. Hence, as a case moves through the various stages of the legal process— complaint, arrest, prosecution, or lawsuit—the stratification of the participants may change, and with it, the fate of the case. A poor man might be indicted on serious charges by the wealthier members of a grand jury, for instance, only to be exonerated later by a jury of his peers. In the same case, a judge with lowly origins might also be more sympathetic than a judge from the higher levels of society. In short, just as law increases with the stratification of the world over the centuries, it increases with the stratification of any relationship at all, even between one person and another, from one day to the next.

VERTICAL LOCATION

If people have an uneven distribution of wealth among them-selves, or stratification, each person or group is higher or lower in relation to others. In this sense, each has a rank, or vertical status. Societies vary in the kinds of wealth they have, however, and so rank depends upon different conditions from one society to another. Simple societies have no private ownership of land, for example, but they may unevenly distribute access to the land or other natural resources of the tribe (see, e.g., Drucker, 1939; Sahlins, 1958:6–7). And the various kinds of wealth in a society may be distributed in different ways in different settings, so that a person or group may have a number of different ranks. Income may be stratified, for example, as in complex societies. The security of wealth may be stratified as well, with some living from day to day, others with investments, savings, and other surplus. Credit, or the ability to borrow wealth, may also be stratified (see Stinchcombe, 1965:171– 172). But no matter how many ranks a person or group has, in any given setting it is always possible to combine these, so that each has a general rank in relation to everyone else.

If people are stratified, it is possible to describe their social life by its location up and down the ranks. It may vary with rank, increasing or decreasing from one to another. This, in fact, applies to law. It is possible to predict and explain the quantity of law with its vertical location:

Law varies directly with rank.

This means that, all else constant, the lower ranks have less law than the higher ranks, and the higher or lower they are, the more or less they have. For these purposes, consider only cases between people of the same rank, since stratified cases have other peculiarities (see next section). Among themselves, then, people with less wealth have less law. They are less likely to call upon law in their dealings with one another, and, when they do, they are less successful.

If a poor man commits a crime against another poor man, for example, this is less serious than if both are wealthy. Less happens. Thus, in the American South during the past century, where blacks generally were of lower rank than whites, a black offending a black was punished less severely than a white offending a white (Johnson, 1941; Myrdal, 1944:550–555). For that matter, the authorities were less likely even to hear about a crime between blacks. The same applies in civil as well as criminal matters. If a poor person kills or otherwise injures another poor person in an automobile accident, for instance, a lawsuit is less likely. And his life or limb is worth less compensation anyway.

In most societies, women and children have less wealth than men, and so they also have less law. In rural Turkey, for instance, women and young people are less likely than men to take each other to court or other legal officials (Starr, 1974:34). In tribal societies, boys who have not been initiated into adulthood generally have less wealth than adults, and so, all else constant, a dispute between uninitiated boys is less likely to result in legal action. If one kills another, it is less serious. In the Anglo-Egyptian Sudan, for example, the Nuer Chiefs' Council held that a killing between uninitiated boys required less compensation than a killing between adult men. If the killing was intentional, or murder, compensation was 20 head of cattle if between uninitiated boys, 40 head if between adult men. If it was an accidental killing between boys, only 10 head of cattle were required, but it was 20 head if this happened between men (Howell, 1954:57).

In modern societies, contact with lawyers varies directly with rank (see Carlin and Howard, 1965:382–383). In the United States, for example, people with higher incomes are more likely to see a lawyer, and so are those who own their own homes (Mayhew and Reiss, 1969:310–311). Many of these visits to lawyers—about one-half— pertain to real estate, wills, or inheritances, matters especially relevant to the lives of wealthier people (Mayhew, 1975:409–410). More lawyers also specialize in the kinds of problems that these people have (Mayhew and Reiss, 1969:317; see also Ladinsky, 1963:54). But, among themselves, wealthier people are more litigious anyway, no matter what their problems are. They are more likely to bring lawsuits against one another for everything, whether fraud, negligence, slander, or divorce.

It might be noted that some persons and groups are themselves property, the wealth of someone else, and their rank should be measured accordingly. On the one hand, they have nothing at all of their own, and yet each is an appendage of an owner with a higher rank. The pure case is the condition of the slave, such as those among the Northwest Coast Indians:

> Slaves, like the natives' dogs, or better still, like canoes and sea otter skins and blankets, were elements of the social configuration but had no active part to play in group life. Their participation was purely passive, like that of a stage-prop carried on and off the boards by the real actors [Drucker, 1939:56].

Not quite so extreme, the slaves of early America were real estate for some purposes, chattels for others, and persons for still others (see, e.g., Hast, 1969). The serfs of medieval Europe were also property for some purposes, but persons for most others (see, e.g., Pollock and Maitland, 1898: Volume 1, 412–432). Dependents of all kinds, including children and women in many societies, are property to some degree. In any case, people such as these have, among themselves, less law than anyone. A slave cannot bring a lawsuit against another slave, for example, even if he so desires. But this does not mean that law has nothing to do with him. On the contrary, like other property, he may be protected against theft, injury, and other offenses. If he is a victim of illegal conduct, however, the offense is against his owner, not him, as in any other offense against property. From a legal standpoint, for instance, an injury to a man's clothing offends the man, not the clothing. And the property itself is not responsible for what happens to it. Thus, among the Basoga of colonial Uganda, only the man was held legally responsible for adultery, since this was a kind of theft. As a Soga chief explained: "You ask why the woman is never the accused in adultery cases. But if someone were to steal your shoes, would you accuse the shoes? [Fallers, 1969:101; see also Fallers, 1956:141–142]." It might be noted that since an offence against human property offends the owner, in such cases the quantity of law varies with the rank of the owner (see page 27).

If, on the other hand, human property does damage or otherwise offends someone else, in the pure case responsibility rests with the owner, whether master, husband, or other guardian. In ancient Athens and Republican Rome, for example, the male head of the household was the only person empowered to own property, and only he had a legal existence:

> The wife and the son could not be plaintiffs or defendants, or accusers, or accused, or witnesses. Of all the family the father alone could appear before the tribunal of the city; public justice existed only for him; and he alone was responsible for the crimes committed by his family [Fustel de Coulanges, 1864:93].

The same applied to a slave (Fustel de Coulanges, 1864:90–93). Similarly, in early English law: "A man was absolutely liable for the acts of his slaves . . . , and a householder was in all probability liable for what was done by the free members of his household [Pollock and Maitland, 1898: Volume 2, 529; see also their page 472]." In eighteenth-century New York City, a master could be fined for his slave's misconduct (Bacon, 1939:98). In modern societies, a parent can be sued for damages done by his child. All of this is the same for the damages of pets or livestock. But damages by one slave against another of the same master, or between children of the same family, are different, since, legally, the offender and victim are the same person, and he does not take legal action against himself.

Groups have wealth as well, and so each group has a rank (see Stinchcombe, 1965:169–174). Hence, law varies directly with the rank of groups, not only among themselves but also in relation to individuals. It is even possible to rank entire societies among themselves, and also the areas of a society, its regions, communities, and neighborhoods. This may be done either according to the distribution of wealth among the residents or according to the wealth of the society or area itself. In the first case, law varies with the proportion of the population that is more or less wealthy. Thus, in the African kingdom of Dahomey, entire communities were inhabited by poor people, and these were largely untouched by law:

> The "bush," i.e., the countryside, retained a social organization that was largely outside the state sphere. The villages where the lower classes lived and the hereditary compounds which enclosed the tilled land and the entailed palm oil trees of the lineages were removed from the action of the central administration. Society as a whole consisted of a state society and a nonstate society [Polanyi, 1966:9].

The same pattern is still seen in many parts of Africa and in Asia, Oceania, and Latin America, wherever enclaves of poverty are found. Similarly, in modern America, black neighborhoods and slums have proportionately less law than white neighborhoods and suburbs (see, e.g., *Yale Law Journal* Editors, 1967:822).

Apart from the distribution of wealth among its inhabitants, the total wealth of a society or community predicts the quantity of its law: The more wealth it has in relation to other societies or communities, the more law it has. Among the societies of traditional Polynesia, for example, the chief's authority increased with the productivity of the society as a whole (Sahlins, 1958: Chapters 2–5; see also page 14). Likewise, the industrialized societies of the world have more law than the less developed societies, such as those of Africa and Latin America. And where one society is the property of another, such as its colony, the owner has more law. People who are

better off materially have more law, then, whether as individuals, groups, communities, or societies.

VERTICAL DIRECTION

Regardless of its vertical location, whether higher or lower, law may have a direction in vertical space. It may move from a higher toward a lower rank, or downward, as well as from a lower to a higher rank, or upward. A complaint by a wealthy man against a poor man has a downward direction, for instance, as does a complaint by a poor man against someone with still less wealth. Correlatively, a complaint has an upward direction whenever it is against someone wealthier than the complainant, regardless of how wealthy each party is. It might be noted that the vertical direction of law is opposite that of deviant behavior: In response to upward deviance law has a downward direction, and in response to downward deviance its direction is upward. Law has vertical direction whenever it moves between different ranks, in civil as well as in criminal matters, and at every stage of a legal process. Legislation may be downward or upward, for example, and the same applies to litigation and adjudication of every kind. What is more, the direction of law in vertical space predicts and explains its quantity:

Downward law is greater than upward law.

This means that, all else constant, law of every kind—whether a statute, complaint, arrest, prosecution, lawsuit, conviction, award of damages, or punishment—is more likely to have a downward direction than an upward direction. It means that upward deviance is more serious than downward deviance.

In the case of a crime, for instance, a victim who is above the offender in rank is more likely to call the police than a victim whose rank is lower than the offender's. In the aggregate, in fact, more calls to the police pertain to upward crimes than to downward crimes. In modern America, for example, the police handle more crimes committed by blacks against whites than the reverse (see Reiss, 1967:53–54), by juveniles against adults than the reverse, and, in general, by poorer people against wealthier people than the reverse.

The same applies to court cases. In Imperial Rome, for example, it was difficult for a man of low rank to gain a hearing for his case against a superior (Garnsey, 1968:7–8). In the New Haven Colony, in seventeenth-century America, the lower ranks made up the majority of the population, but the court handled more downward than upward complaints (Baumgartner, 1975:27). And, over time, as complaints turn toward the higher ranks, law may even retreat from its former jurisdiction. Thus, in the Massachusetts Bay Colony, witch trials came to a halt when the accusations turned upward:

> The net of accusation was beginning to spread out in wider arcs, reaching not only across the surface of the country but up the social ladder as well, so that a number of influential people were now among those in the overflowing prisons . . . . Slowly but surely, a faint glimmer of skepticism was introduced into the situation . . . . The afflicted girls . . . were beginning to display an ambition which far exceeded their credit. It was bad enough that they should accuse the likes of John Alden and Nathanial Cary, but when they brought up the name of Samuel Willard, who doubled as pastor of Boston's First Church and President of Harvard College, the magistrates flatly told them they were mistaken [Erikson, 1966:148, 149].

It is also more difficult to win an upward than a downward case. In the Congo (now Zaire), for instance, where Pygmies were treated as the personal property of Bantus, a Pygmy could never win:

> [The chief of the BaNdaka] did not consider the Pygmies real people, and therefore they had no right to have cases tried in the tribunal. He said that any complaints by the [Bantu] villagers against Pygmies were heard by him; he judged them himself and no records were kept. He made it quite plain that the judgment always went in favor of the villager [Turnbull, 1961:234].

In Imperial Rome, also, the party of higher rank had an advantage:

> Even if the plaintiff of low rank had been granted an action, and had secured the appearance of his opponent before the praetor [a court officer], he could not have had much confidence in the outcome of the action. For a man of influence would stand a good chance of winning his case, even without corruption or the threat of force. Judges and juries (where there were juries)

were easily impressed by qualities such as social prominence, wealth and good character, and this was thought perfectly proper [Garnsey, 1968:9].

In the New Haven Colony as well, the party of higher rank was more likely to win (Baumgartner, 1975:40). And today, in rural Mexico, the elite is nearly immune to people at the bottom: "Lower-class individuals seldom bring a case to court in the hope of winning, unless their opponent is an even match in wealth and power [Hunt and Hunt, 1969:123]." To one degree or another, the same principle applies everywhere. It might be added that a judge or other official higher in rank than a litigant is less likely to find merit in his case. In a trial by jury, a party to a case has a disadvantage if the jury members are wealthier than he, but an advantage if they are beneath him. At every stage, in every legal setting, a downward case is stronger than an upward case.

Compensation and punishment also vary accordingly. In ancient Babylonia, for instance, the Code of Hammurabi explicitly recognized the vertical direction of an offense:

If a man strike another man of his own rank, he shall pay one mana of silver.

If a man strike the person of a man . . . who is his superior, he shall receive sixty strokes with an ox-tail whip in public . . . .

If a man's slave strike a man's son, they shall cut off his ear [Harper, 1904: Sections 203, 202, 205].

In traditional India, murder and certain other offenses against a man higher in caste were punishable by death, but Brahmans, the highest caste, and any murderer of a man lower in caste, were exempt from this penalty (Gough, 1960:48). In fifteenth-century Peru, a crime against an Inca, or aristocrat, was more serious than other crime (Moore, 1958:82). In Manchu China, "violence against a superior was punished more severely than violence to an inferior [van der Sprenkel, 1962:27]."

More recently, in Australian Papua, a native who raped or attempted to rape a white woman was subject to a mandatory death penalty, provided by the "White Women's Protection Ordinance" of 1926 (see Inglis, 1974: Chapter 3). But a white man who sexually assaulted a native woman was, for all practical purposes, immune to law: "It would have been almost impossible for a Papuan to win a case against a white man [Inglis, 1974:79]." In South Africa, where whites rank above nonwhites, interracial law also varies with its vertical direction. Thus, downward rape or murder is less serious than upward rape or murder:

> Analysis of sentences imposed for cross-color rape and murder over a recent period of three years for which information is available, 1957–59 inclusive, shows that no white was sentenced to death for the rape or murder of a non-white in that period, while at least 37 and 13 non-whites were executed for the crimes of murder and rape, respectively, against whites.

> Certain facts are clear over a longer period. No white has ever been executed for the rape of a non-white woman. Since 1960, two whites have been executed for rape: in both cases the victims were white as well. Whites convicted of raping non-white women generally receive sentences of imprisonment which rarely exceed five years. Execution of a non-white for the rape of a white woman is, however, the general rule [Welsh, 1969:416].

In the United States as well, the punishment of rape, murder, and other crimes follows the same principle (e.g., Johnson, 1941; Garfinkel, 1949; see also Rubin, 1966:65–67; Hagan, 1974:370–373). It might be noted that comparisons such as these should be made according to the offender's actual conduct, rather than according to the crime with which he is charged, since the charge itself is a variable aspect of law (compare, e.g., Green, 1964). An upward crime is more likely to receive a serious charge. By every measure, then, upward crimes are more serious than downward crimes.

*　*　*

Among cases with direction between one rank and another, the difference between the ranks, or vertical distance, also predicts and explains the quantity of law. But this depends upon the direction of law in each case. Downward law increases with this distance, whereas the behavior of upward law is just the opposite:

Downward law varies directly with vertical distance.

But:

Upward law varies inversely with vertical distance.

The seriousness of an offense by a lower against a higher rank thus increases with the difference in wealth between the parties, whereas the seriousness of an offense by a higher against a lower rank decreases as this difference increases. Hold the victim's rank constant, then, and law varies inversely with the offender's rank. The wealthier a thief is, for instance, the less serious is his theft. Thus, in modern America, department stores are less likely to prosecute shoplifters who are middle-class and white than those who are lower-class and black, and, in court, the same applies to the likelihood of conviction, a jail sentence, and a sentence of 30 days or more (Cameron, 1964:136–143). And when their own employees steal from them, they are more lenient toward those with better jobs (Robin, 1967:693). Whatever the crime, wealth is an advantage for the offender (see, e.g., Wiseman, 1970:90; Mileski, 1971:507–508). This applies where the victim's rank is constant, or where, for these purposes, it may be assumed to be so. In some legal settings, in fact, a wealthier offender may directly buy an advantage for himself in one way or another. In medieval Europe, for instance, he could buy a champion at law to fight for him in a trial by combat (see, e.g., Pollock and Maitland, 1898: Volume 2, 633). Similarly, in some societies he may buy a lawyer, or a better lawyer than others can afford (comparison drawn by Hobhouse, 1951:122). But a lawyer who represents a wealthier client is more likely to win anyway.

Even if convicted and sentenced, a man of higher rank has other advantages. He is more likely to be pardoned or paroled, for instance. If imprisoned, he is more likely to have privileges. Thus, in the British colony of the Gold Coast (now Ghana), the prison rules specified that in addition to the ration of fish and corn for blacks, white prisoners would receive a half pound of bread, meat, or fowl three times a week, a pound of fish four times a week, two eggs and a half pound of rice daily, along with tea and sugar (Seidman, 1969:467, note 39). In the New Haven Colony, a wealthier offender was less likely to be executed (Baumgartner, 1972), and also less likely to be put in the stocks for public ridicule, whipped, or degraded in other ways (Baumgartner, 1975:43–46). In many societies, wealth can be paid as compensation in place of punishment or as a fine in place of more severe punishment. In modern America, money can be paid in place of detention before trial and, in some cases, in place of a jail sentence. In many societies, a wealthier offender is subject to less severity even when condemned to death: He is less likely to be tortured or humiliated on the day of his execution. In Imperial Rome, for example, execution of an upper-class offender was never more severe than decapitation, the gentlest method. A lower-class offender, however, was subject to such methods as exposure to wild beasts, burning, and crucifixion (Garnsey, 1968:13). In the African kingdom of Nupe, a man of rank was allowed to be killed at night and in his own home, whereas a commoner's execution was a public spectacle in the marketplace (Nadel, 1942:167).

Now assume that the offender's rank is constant, and law varies directly with the rank of the victim. In traditional India, for instance, the seriousness of an offense increased with the caste of the victim:

> The amount of internal pollution ego incurs is proportionate to the purity of his victim's *varna* [caste]; for example, the penance for killing a Kshatriya [second rank] is less than that for killing a Brahman [first rank], and so on down in *varna* rank. Defilement is simply dependent upon the magnitude of the crime, which depends, in turn, upon the purity of the victim [Orenstein, 1968:116].

This was not merely a matter of religious ritual, but was expressed in worldly punishments as well (see page 23 of this volume). The sex of the victim was also important. In one code, for example, the murder of a Brahman woman was only as serious as the murder of a Kshatriya man, and so on down the ranks (Orenstein, 1968:125).

Compensation also increases with the rank of the victim. The wealthier he is, the greater is the damage. Among the Tlingit Indians of the Northwest Coast, for instance, this was established by tradition:

> Individual families are ranked; they form a sort of aristocracy which bases its position not so much on birth as on the possession of wealth. Even the rank

of chief is tied up with the possession of wealth, largely the ownership of slaves . . . . For the death or injury of an important person greater compensation is demanded than for a person of lesser rank; two or more lives being payment for one chief [Krause, 1885:77, 84].

A payment scale of this kind also appeared in the early law of England, where the payment was known as a *wergild,* or man's price (see, e.g., Pike, 1873:49; Pollock and Maitland, 1898: Volume 1, 33, 47–48; Volume 2, 451). In modern America as well, compensation for personal injuries varies directly with the rank of the victim: The wealthier he is, the more compensation he or his survivors receive. For that matter, a wealthier victim is more likely to demand compensation. Thus, an accidental injury to a wealthier person is more likely to be defined and litigated as a case of negligence. In the case of an automobile accident involving major personal injuries, a wealthier victim is more likely to hire a lawyer (Conard, Morgan, Pratt, Voltz, and Bombaugh, 1964:226–227; also see Carlin and Howard, 1965:424–425; Mayhew and Reiss, 1969:310–311). And he is more likely to file a lawsuit against the driver of the other automobile (Conard *et al.,* 1964:257–258). If the victim is the dependent of a wealthier man, such as his wife or child, this is more serious as well. If his child is accidentally killed, for instance, this is worse than the death of a poor man's child: Compensation varies directly with the wealth of the parent. And a wealthier parent is more likely to ask for compensation in the first place.

Hold constant the offender's rank, and wealthier people complain more about everything. In criminal matters, for instance, the likelihood of a call to the police increases with the rank of the victim. So does the likelihood of a complaint about the police themselves, such as a complaint of "police brutality" (Chevigny, 1969:xviii), about racial discrimination (Mayhew, 1968:155–159), or about business practices (see Steele, 1975:1123–1126). The more people have, the more litigious they are, and the more success they have with their litigation as well (see generally Carlin, Howard, and Messinger, 1966; compare Galanter, 1974). The wealthier the victim of a crime, the more likely is an investigation by the police (see Black, 1970:745–746), an arrest, prosecution, conviction, and punishment. In civil matters, the wealthier the plaintiff, the better is his case.

People with nothing at all may not even be allowed to complain. Among the Basoga of Uganda, for example, a woman could not sue for divorce:

> Traditionally, a woman herself cannot bring a divorce action, . . . and her incompetence in this respect is bound up with her whole position in society. A woman, in Soga society, must always live as a dependent of, and under the authority of a man: her father before she is married, her husband afterwards [Fallers, 1956:141].

The same applied to women and other dependents in many societies of the past, including ancient Greece and Rome (Fustel de Coulanges, 1864:90–94). Thus, law generally does not protect a slave, not even his life, against his owner (e.g., Fustel de Coulanges, 1864:93; Krause, 1885:105). In fact, if a Roman slave accused his owner of any crime other than treason, this accusation was itself a crime and the slave was condemned to gladiatorial combat in the arena (Pike, 1873:14).

*   *   *

It is possible to order the seriousness of deviant behavior according to its vertical location and direction, at once. All else constant, upward deviance is the most serious, followed by deviant behavior between people of high rank, then between people of low rank, and finally by downward deviance. The quantity of law decreases accordingly, and this applies to law of every kind. In cases of homicide, for example, the most severe punishment befalls a poor man who kills a wealthy man, followed by a wealthy man who kills another equally wealthy, then a poor man whose victim is equally poor, while the least severe punishment is given to a wealthy man who kills a poor man (see Johnson, 1941; Garfinkel, 1949).

It should be noted that the quantity of law in a vertical case, whether downward or upward, also varies with its vertical location, whether higher or lower. This is an implication of the principle that law varies directly with rank (see page 17). All else constant, then, law is greater in a downward case where both parties are comparatively wealthy than in a downward case where both are comparatively poor. And the same applies to cases in the opposite direction.

* * *

Stratification also predicts and explains the style of law, whether it is penal, compensatory, therapeutic, or conciliatory. For example: Downward law is more penal than upward law. In other words, where the offender's rank is below the victim's, his conduct is more likely to be punished as a crime than in a case where the direction is the opposite, with the victim's rank below the offender's. Upward law is more compensatory than downward law. Thus, an offender who ranks above his victim is more likely to be asked to pay for his damage than in a case with the opposite direction. Upward law is also more therapeutic than downward law. Where an offender against his superior may be punished, for instance, an offender against an inferior is more likely to be defined as sick and in need of treatment. If a wealthy man takes property from poor people, he may be asked to give back what he expropriated or he may be hospitalized as mentally ill, but he is less likely to be punished as a criminal than a poor man who takes from the rich.

The style of law varies with vertical distance as well: In a downward direction, penal law varies directly with vertical distance, and in an upward direction it varies inversely with vertical distance. The wealthier a victim in relation to his offender, then, the more likely is the penal style of law. But the wealthier an offender in relation to his victim, the less likely this is. If the offender is wealthier, however, compensatory and therapeutic law become ever more likely as his wealth is greater. Hold constant the victim's rank, and penal law varies inversely with the offender's rank. And, under the same conditions, compensatory and therapeutic law vary directly with the offender's rank (see Aubert and Messinger, 1958:40–43). With the offender's rank constant, on the other hand, the penal style of law varies directly with the victim's rank, and the compensatory and therapeutic styles vary inversely with his rank.

Finally, it might be noted that vertical law of either kind, whether downward or upward, is less conciliatory than law between people who are equal in rank. In other words: Conciliatory law varies inversely with stratification. This means that equals, whether high or low in rank, are more likely to work out a compromise than are people with different ranks. And the greater the difference between them, the less conciliatory they are. As the stratification of a community or society increases, then, conciliation declines, replaced ever more by punishment, compensation, or treatment. Over the centuries and across the world, the style of law fluctuates with the distribution of wealth.

DEPRIVATION AND DEVIANT BEHAVIOR

One theory of deviant behavior holds that an individual who is deprived of wealth is more likely to deviate. Deprivation leads to frustration, which in turn explains the motivation to engage in deviant behavior (see, e.g., Bonger, 1916: Part 2, Book 2, Chapters 1–2; Dollard, Miller, Doob, Mowrer, and Sears, 1939: Chapter 6). One version, for example, holds that an individual deprived of the legitimate means to improve his condition is more likely to use illegitimate means, such as theft or illicit business (e.g., Merton, 1938a; Cloward and Ohlin, 1960). Another holds that an individual who suffers deprivation is more likely to engage in conduct that is aggressive or destructive, such as violence or vandalism (e.g., Henry and Short, 1954; Cohen, 1955). It might also be noted that deprivation theory typically locates the motivation to deviate in the deprivation of an individual in relation to others, not in his absolute deprivation. Hence, it is an individual's rank that ultimately predicts his deviant behavior.

If deviant behavior is understood as conduct that is subject to social control (see page 9), many facts support deprivation theory. In the case of crime and juvenile delinquency in the United States, for example, official records show that poor people contribute more than their share of offenders: They are more likely to be arrested, prosecuted, convicted, and sent to prison or a reformatory (see, e.g., Sutherland and Cressey, 1960:189–193; Reiss and Rhodes, 1961;

Shaw and McKay, 1969:147–152). The same is true of crime and delinquency in other societies (e.g., Bonger, 1916: Part 2, Book 2, Chapters 2–4; Sutherland and Cressey, 1960:191). It is important to note, however, that this applies only to conduct that is vulnerable to law when it is detected, not to that which merely appears illegal even though it is not actually handled as such. In this sense, much so-called "unreported crime" and "unrecorded crime" is not crime at all, including, for instance, much "white-collar crime" and "middle-class delinquency" (compare, e.g., Sutherland, 1945; Nye, Short, and Olson, 1958; Ennis, 1967; Hirschi, 1969:66–75; but see, e.g., Kitsuse and Cicourel, 1963; Turk, 1969:8–18). In short, deprivation theory predicts who is actually subject to law.

The theory of law predicts these facts as well. As criminal law varies across social settings, so, by definition, does crime, since crime is conduct that is subject to criminal law. Thus, since downward law is greater than upward law (see page 21), it follows that upward crime is more likely than downward crime. And since downward law varies directly with vertical distance, whereas upward law varies inversely with this distance (see pages 24–25), it follows that, with the victim's rank constant, criminality varies inversely with rank. It might be noted that these principles apply whatever the actual conduct of the lower ranks—whether, for example, it is more or less violent or predatory—since their conduct is more likely to be defined as illegal no matter what they do. It might also be noted that the penal style of law, as in criminal law, is especially likely under these conditions (see page 29). The theory of law therefore predicts and explains the higher rate of crime among people who are deprived of wealth. It predicts the same facts as deprivation theory, then, but explains these facts without regard to the motivation of the deviant. One explains crime with the behavior of the criminal, the other with the behavior of law.

THE BEHAVIOR OF SOCIAL CONTROL

Stratification explains not only law but social control of every kind, formal and informal, public and private, traditional and modern (see Moore, 1942). Each varies with the quantity of stratification, and with its own location and direction in vertical space.

Social control in a family, for example, increases with the inequality of wealth among its members. Thus, in a monogamous society, the authority of the father varies directly with the dependency of his wife and children. In societies where the sons have little or nothing of their own until their father's death, for instance, as in aristocracies and many other agrarian societies, the father's authority is greater than where the sons become independent at an early age, as in modern societies (see Tocqueville, 1840:584–589; Demos, 1970a:103, 164–170). And in any family with stratification, more social control flows downward than upward. In an aristocratic family, for instance, more social control flows not only from the father, but also from the eldest son:

> In the aristocratic family the eldest son, who will inherit most of the property and almost all the rights, becomes the chief and to a certain extent the master of his brothers. Greatness and power are his; for them there is mediocrity and dependence [Tocqueville, 1840:588].

It might be noted that in modern as well as in aristocratic societies most wives are dependent upon the wealth of their husbands, and so, in general, they are criticized and disciplined more by their husbands than are their husbands by them. This difference decreases as the income and other wealth of the wife increases, and with equality it disappears.

Social control in organizations and other groups also varies with stratification. The greater the differences in income among the employees of a business, for instance, the more bureaucratic it is (see page 101). This varies with rank as well, with the higher-ups having more social control among themselves than those below. But those below often are subject to discipline from above, whereas little or no social control flows upward. In a school, the wealthier students are subject to less social control. If they do get into trouble, their excuses are more likely to be accepted (see Blumstein, 1974), and, in any case, their punishments are less severe.

On the other hand, if a wealthier person is victimized by someone else, he is more likely to complain, and his complaint is more likely to succeed. This applies to social control in settings of all kinds. If he is the victim of an automobile accident, for example, a wealthier man receives more compensation from the insurance company, and with less delay as well (Hunting and Neuwirth, 1962:150).

Now, finally, consider etiquette, a kind of social control that appears in every social setting, wherever people come together. Etiquette is the social control of face-to-face interaction as such, of meetings, greetings, and forms of address; invitations, entrances, and departures; gestures, postures, expressions, and intonations (see generally Goffman, 1956; 1963; 1971). It defines what is proper and what is not, what is mannerly and rude, graceful and vulgar, kind, considerate, interested, detached, tactless, oblivious, or cold. The quantity of etiquette is known by the prohibitions, obligations, and other standards to which people are subject, and by responses to breach. Etiquette varies in style as well, with punishment of the deviant in some cases, an apology from him in others, pity for his condition in still others. In quantity as well as in style, moreover, it varies with the distribution of wealth.

Etiquette varies directly with stratification. For instance, aristocratic societies have more than do societies with a wider circulation of wealth:

> There is too much mobility in the population of a democracy for any definite group to be able to establish a code of behavior and see that it is observed. So everyone behaves more or less after his own fashion, and a certain incoherence of manners always prevails . . . . In aristocracies rules of propriety impose the same demeanor on all, making every member of the same class seem alike in spite of personal characteristics . . . . Democratic manners are neither so well thought out nor so regular [Tocqueville, 1840:606, 607].

Similarly, in traditional Polynesia, etiquette between chief and commoner increased with the stratification of a society. At one extreme, for instance, was Ontong Java, one of the least stratified of these societies, and there taboos protecting the *mana*, or sacredness, of chiefs operated only when they were officiating at tribal ceremonies (see Sahlins, 1958: 97–100, 105). At another extreme was Hawaii, one of the most stratified, and here numerous taboos protected the chief at all times. A commoner could not touch a chief or his possessions, for example, not even with his shadow, everyone was required to prostrate himself on the ground in the presence of the chief, and the ground over which he walked was sacred as well (Sahlins, 1958:20–21). The same applies elsewhere. Thus, families with more stratification have more formalities of every kind, pre- scribed manner of dress, speech, seating at meals, and forms of address. The same is true of organizations. Just as bureaucracy in- creases with the stratification of a business or other organization, so does etiquette: Some are allowed a more relaxed demeanor than others, for instance, and some are called by their first names, but not others.

Etiquette also varies directly with rank. Among themselves, the higher ranks have more than the lower ranks. They have more table manners, more taboo topics in conversations, more rules of decorum of all kinds (see Goffman, 1959b:133). Thus, among themselves, aristocrats have more etiquette than peasants, adults more than chil- dren, masters more than slaves or other servants. Among the Maori of New Zealand, for example, a man's rank could be surmised from the way he ate his food:

> A *rangatira* or well-born person could always be detected by his manner of eating. Given a bird, fish or rat, he would always commence at the head, cleaning the bones thoroughly as he worked along . . . . If fresh bones were found in the bush a native could always tell, by the manner in which they had been picked, whether a chief or a commoner had feasted; also, a well-bred man would keep his hands perfectly clean when eating [Downes, 1929:153].

The higher ranks expect one another to pay more attention to their clothing as well, and to grooming, hospitality, and other kinds of courtesy, including that of their children and other dependents. This is "polite society." Here there are stricter rules of privacy, of who may visit whom, under what conditions, concerning which occa- sions, and for how long. In modern America, for instance:

> The household planning and preparation for visits which are so prominent in more affluent neighborhoods [are] almost entirely lacking [in the slum] . . . . Telephone calls are seldom made before people "drop in." Advance in- vitations are even more uncommon . . . . Formal gatherings tend to be equally rare; cocktail parties, formal dinners, teas, and invitational parties are almost unheard of [Suttles, 1968:77].

Rules of privacy include the regulation of territoriality of all kinds, such as who may touch whom and how close each may approach the other (see generally Lyman and Scott, 1967). Privacy varies directly with rank. In a modern society, for example, etiquette demands more physical distance between the higher ranks:

> Here . . . is one of the important differences between social classes in our society: not only are some of the tokens different through which consideration for the privacy of others is expressed, but also, apparently, the higher the class the more extensive and elaborate are the taboos against contact. For example, in a study of a Shetlandic community the writer found that as one moves from middle-class urban centers in Britain to the rural lower-class islands, the distance between chairs at table decreases, so that in the outermost Shetland Islands actual body contact during meals and similar social occasions is not considered an invasion of separateness and no effort need be made to excuse it [Goffman, 1956:481].

Children among themselves also have less privacy of this kind, and women have less than men.

When people of different ranks intermingle, however, etiquette varies with its vertical direction: Downward etiquette is greater than upward etiquette. In other words, etiquette demands more from the lower ranks in relation to their superiors than from those above in relation to their inferiors. An example is the deference expected of a subject toward his monarch, or of a servant toward his master. In the Old South, for instance, a slave was expected to touch his hat upon meeting a white person, whereas a white did not have an obligation of this kind. If a conversation arose, the slave was expected to remove his hat and keep his eyes on the ground, and he could not eat, drink, or sit in the presence of his master (Doyle, 1937:13–14, 19–20). In general, a person of higher rank is permitted to be more relaxed when in the presence of his inferiors. What is improper for an inferior may even be defined as a virtue of someone higher up:

> Charm and colorful little informalities are . . . usually the prerogatives of those in higher office, leading us mistakenly to assume that an individual's social graces helped bring him to his high position, instead of what is perhaps more likely, that the graces become possible for anyone who attains the office [Goffman, 1961b:129].

At the staff meetings of a mental hospital, for example:

> Medical doctors had the privilege of swearing, changing the topic of conversation, and sitting in undignified positions; attendants, on the other hand,

had the right to attend staff meetings . . . but were implicitly expected to conduct themselves with greater circumspection than was required of doctors [Goffman, 1956:490].

A person of higher rank may also be permitted a greater degree of intimacy toward his inferiors. Thus, in modern America, a medical doctor may call a nurse by her first name, but she must be more formal, and the same applies to his patients—at least those of lower rank. The same applies to a businessman and his secretary, an adult and children, and many others (see Goffman, 1956:481–482). Liberties with the privacy of inferiors may be allowed as well, so that a ship's captain may freely enter the territory of ordinary seamen, or "fo'c'sle," but they may not enter his, and the same applies to a military officer in relation to his men or, to a lesser degree, a parent in relation to his child (Goffman, 1961b:129; Schwartz, 1968:743, 748–749). A superior may even have access to the persons of those below, the right to touch or handle them, as when an adult tousles a child's hair (see Goffman, 1956:487). On the other hand, a person of lower rank who does not keep his distance from a superior may be considered disrespectful (see Simmel, 1908b:321–322).

A breach of etiquette by a lower against a higher rank is more serious than a breach in the opposite direction. A person must be more polite toward his superiors than toward his peers, and less so toward his inferiors. So, in modern America, face-to-face social control such as eyebrow raising, tongue clicking, head shaking, staring, snorting, and scolding is greater in a downward than an upward direction. A faux pas, even vulgarity, by a superior is more likely to be ignored entirely. A superior may have his idiosyncrasies. And the higher his rank in relation to the person he offends, the more he is allowed (see Hollander, 1958; 1960). The style of etiquette also varies with stratification. A breach at the expense of a superior is more likely to be punished, for example, whereas a downward breach is more likely to be compensated. Thus, in a modern society, a child who is rude to an adult may be punished in one way or another, but in the case of an adult who is rude to a child, an apology is usually enough.

3

MORPHOLOGY

Morphology is the horizontal aspect of social life, the distribution of people in relation to one another, including their division of labor, networks of interaction, intimacy, and integration (compare Sorokin, 1927: 7–10). It varies across social settings of every kind, whether societies, communities, neighborhoods, or organizations, public places or events, marriages or friendships. It varies across time as well, from century to century and day to day. One village or tribe may have a greater division of labor—more differentiation— than another, and this also applies to factories, universities, families, and teams. Some settings are intimate, others impersonal. In some, nearly everyone participates in everything; in others, many are marginal or alone.

Morphological variables explain many of the patterns of social life. For example, increasing differentiation over the centuries explains many other patterns of social evolution, such as the attenuation of the family, the growth of government, and the diversification of cultural life (see Spencer, 1876: Part 2; Tönnies, 1887; Durkheim, 1893; Parsons, 1966). Differentiation also explains aspects of stratification (Davis and Moore, 1945), religion (Swanson, 1960: Chapter 4), violence (Durkheim, 1950: Chapter 10), and organization (Udy, 1959:

Chapter 3; Blau, 1970:13–18). And other morphological variables explain other aspects of social life, such as patterns of sociability (Simmel, 1908b:111–114), joking (Radcliffe-Brown, 1940), and intellectual life, including science (Durkheim and Mauss, 1903; Berger and Kellner, 1964; Crane, 1972).

Morphology also explains the quantity and style of law. This strategy of explanation has been applied to the evolution of law (Maine, 1861:161–165; Tönnies, 1887: Part 3; Durkheim, 1893) as well as to other patterns such as litigation and adjudication (Gulliver, 1963:258–267; Nader, 1965; Gluckman, 1967:19–21). It is possible to formulate general propositions that imply many earlier explanations, that order known facts, and that predict numerous patterns yet to be observed. It is possible to explain law with differentiation, with intimacy, and with the location and direction of law itself in relation to the center of social life.

THE QUANTITY OF DIFFERENTIATION

Differentiation is a specialization of function across the parts of a whole. Some kinds of life have a great deal of differentiation, with many organs linked to one another, each useless without the rest, whereas others have many identical parts, each doing the same thing, with little interdependence among them. Compare a protozoan to a flatworm, crustacean, bird, or man. Differentiation also varies across groups. For instance, social insects, such as bees and ants, have more than other insects. Among people, differentiation varies across settings of every kind, from societies to organizations, families, and friendships. Since it might at first seem otherwise, it should be noted that differentiation is not simply a function of the size of a population. In many cases social life differentiates as population increases (see Durkheim, 1893: Book 2, Chapter 2), but in some it involutes, multiplying without diversifying, growing without developing (see Goldenweiser, 1936:102–104). Involution may occur in many aspects of social life, including the economic life of societies with rapidly increasing populations (see Geertz, 1963:70–82, 96–97). Within a society as well, smaller groups may display more differentiation than larger groups.

Law varies directly with differentiation, to a point, then reverses itself:

The relationship between law and differentiation is curvilinear.

Specifically, law increases with differentiation to a point of interdependence but declines with symbiosis. There is less law where people are undifferentiated by function, with little or no exchange among themselves, and, at the other extreme, where each is completely dependent upon the next.

Consider, for example, the law of economic life, such as contract law, property law, and the criminal law pertaining to matters of ownership and exchange. In simple societies such as nomadic bands and herdsmen, each family engages in much the same productive activity as the next. Exchanges of property and services are uncommon and, in any case, are personal as well as economic transactions. Under these conditions, a law of contract does not exist (see, e.g., Ghai, 1969). As labor divides, however, economic transactions become a part of daily life separate from personal relationships, and law increases. This has happened over the centuries in some places, in decades or years in others. Hence, the state and law expand with the market (see, e.g., Weber, 1925: Chapter 6; Parsons, 1966; Sanders, 1968; Johnson, 1973). Especially noticeable, for instance, is the evolution of property law (Durkheim, 1950:171) and the law of theft (Hall, 1952:62–79). All manner of legal agencies and officials appear, as differentiated as the people they regulate. By the early nineteenth century, for example, all of these offices had appeared in New York City:

inspectors of tobacco, inspectors of flour, inspectors of weights and measures, captains of boats, surveyors and gaugers of casks, overseers of butchers, inspectors of the transporting of liquors, overseers of carts and cartmen, haven masters, clerks of the markets, inspectors of pipe staves, inspectors of leather, inspectors of grain for distilling, weighers of loaf bread, packers and viewers of casks, inspectors of horses and cattle for export, weighmasters for hay, inspectors of firewood, inspectors of boards, inspectors of flax, inspectors of places selling liquor, measurers of lime, measurers of grain, repackers of beef and pork, measurers of ship timber, gaugers of liquors and liquids, inspectors of hemp, inspectors of pot and pearl ash, inspectors of sole leather, measurers of charcoal, inspectors of manure, inspectors of fish, inspectors of lumber, inspectors of hackney carriages, superintendents of stages, inspectors of pawn shops, superintendents of junk shops, weighers of anthracite coal [Bacon, 1939:767].

There were others as well, including some not tied so obviously to the division of labor, such as night police, animal police, Sunday police, and epidemic police (Bacon, 1939:781). To a point, moreover, as the division of labor increases, so does the severity of law: "Severe punishments are found more frequently in relatively differentiated societies, while simple societies are more likely to be characterized by lenient forms [Spitzer, 1975:624; compare Durkheim, 1899–1900:32]." As social life evolves beyond interdependence to symbiosis, however, law decreases.

Law also varies with the degree of differentiation across the settings of a society at any given point in time. In the business world, for example, law is greater where people are interdependent but not symbiotic. In fact, many exchange relationships in capitalistic societies are symbiotic to a degree, such as where manufacturers form a chain of production and consumption, each helpless without the others, and in these cases law is comparatively dormant (see, e.g., Macaulay, 1963). The same applies to a lesser degree where dependency is not mutual, as in pure symbiosis, but one-sided, such as where a distributor has only one supplier while the supplier has numerous distributors (see, e.g., Kessler, 1957; Macaulay, 1966), or where a sales relationship has only one potential seller or condition of sale so that the buyer has no choice (see Kessler, 1943). Instead, law is more likely in a true market setting, where each needs the other but has alternatives as well (see Durkheim, 1893:206–219). This even applies to the community of nations: International law increases with the division of labor across the world (see Deutsch, 1968), declining only with symbiosis.

RELATIONAL DISTANCE

People vary in the degree to which they participate in one another's lives. This defines their intimacy, or relational distance (compare, e.g., Park, 1924; Sorokin, 1927:6–8). The closest relationships involve total interpenetration, the most distant none at all. It is possible to measure relational distance in many ways, including the scope, frequency, and length of interaction between people, the age of their relationship, and the nature and number of links between them in a social network (see Mitchell, 1969:12–20; Granovetter, 1973: 1366, note 10). Just as it is possible to measure the stratification of many people in relation to one another (see page 13), so the intimacy of a larger setting may be measured by the relational distance, on the average, between each person or group and every other, and by the range between the people who are farthest apart.

Relational distance predicts and explains the quantity of law:

> *The relationship between law and*
> *relational distance is curvilinear.*

Law is inactive among intimates, increasing as the distance between people increases but decreasing as this reaches the point at which people live in entirely separate worlds. In a modern society, relational distance rarely reaches the point where people are entirely separate, but it is greater than in simpler societies. Modernization destroys the closeness of tribal and other traditional settings, weakening kinship and other communal relationships. At the same time, however, it draws people together, combining worlds that were once separate. People increasingly become strangers to each other, but this is a relationship in itself:

> The unity of nearness and remoteness involved in every human relation is organized, in the phenomenon of the stranger, in a way which may be most briefly formulated by saying that in the relationship to him, distance means that he, who is close by, is far, and strangeness means that he, who also is far, is actually near. For, to be a stranger is naturally a very positive relation; it is a specific form of interaction. The inhabitants of Sirius are not really strangers to us, at least not in any sociologically relevant sense: they do not exist for us at all; they are beyond far and near. The stranger, like the poor and like sundry "inner enemies," is an element of the group itself. His position as a full-fledged member involves both being outside it and confronting it . . . . In spite of being inorganically appended to it, the stranger is yet an organic member of the group [Simmel, 1908b:402–403, 408].

And in the midst of strangers, law reaches its highest level.

First consider the upward slope of the curve: All else constant, a person is least likely to sue a close kinsman, then a friend, an acquaintance, a neighbor, a fellow tribesman, a fellow townsman, and so on, the likelihood increasing with relational distance until his world ends. Among the Arusha of colonial Tanganyika (now Tanzania), for example, disputes between closely related people, such as members of the same family line or village, almost always were handled with procedures not involving the government. Only those more distant were likely to go to law: "Courts deal with disputes between men who are distantly linked patrilineally, and who live more than a few miles apart [Gulliver, 1963:204, italics omitted]." Similar patterns appeared among other tribes of colonial Africa (e.g., Bohannan, 1957:210; Tanner, 1966:7). In traditional Japan as well, where intimacy extended to the village boundaries, fellow villagers avoided court, but members of different villages did not (Kawashima, 1963:43–45). In a modern society, with people moving from place to place, from one large organization or city to another, strangers are encountered everywhere, and law is an ever-present possibility. But little law enters the sanctuaries of intimacy. Thus, intimates are less likely to call the police about each other (see McIntyre, 1967:45; Block, 1974:560–561). If they do, the police are less likely to handle their problem as a crime (Black, 1970:740–741), and, in any case, they are less likely to make an arrest (Black, 1971:1097–1098). If an intimate is arrested, he is less likely to be prosecuted (Hall, 1952:318). In fact, an intimate's associates may shield him from the law: They are less likely to cooperate with the investigation of his offense; they are more likely to lie for him; they are more likely to hide him. The court may even excuse family members from testifying against each other. In many ways, then, intimacy provides immunity from law.

At the other extreme, equally immune from law, are the people who live in different worlds, more distant than strangers. Typically people this far apart also live in different cultures, in different tribes or nations, but this need not be the case. Among the Basseri of South Persia, for example, two ways of life coexist, herding and farming, one nomadic, the other sedentary. Although they share a language, religion, and many customs, the demands of herding, with its constant movement for the sake of the animals, entirely separates the nomad from the farmer. Conflict between the two is possible, such as when a nomad's herd damages a farmer's crops, but it is conflict in a social vacuum, between people who share no social system. Hence, although law appears from time to time among the nomads, and among the farmers, it does not appear between them:

> The opponents in a conflict between a nomad and a farmer cannot maintain contact for long; the difference in their modes of life precludes all the activities usually associated with mediation and the settlement of conflicts. Left to their own devices they can only mobilize their own communities and fight it out—and the prevalence of fortified villages in Southern Fars bears evidence to the frequency of this resort in the past, and its occasional practice today [Barth, 1961:79; see also 74–78].

Even a single locality of a traditional society may divide into separate worlds, with the people of each entirely independent, rarely seeing each other, and never interacting. This may involve different ethnic groups, but it also happens in other ways. In Lebanon, for instance, two large families live almost completely apart in the isolated village of Libaya:

> Libaya is a village which for as long as anyone can remember has been split into two opposing factions based on family alliances—one headed by the Akls, and the other by the Abrahams. Each faction (except for the rare marriage by capture) is endogamous . . . . All the recreative as well as political activities and family or life cycle activities are patterned along lines of this dual division [Nader, 1965:395].

With this much relational distance between its halves and so little within each, it is not surprising that Libaya has little law, in fact, no police or court of its own (see Nader, 1965:395). With respect to its distant segments, this is not unlike a relationship between hostile tribes or subtribes or, for that matter, an international relationship (see Hoebel, 1954:331; Barkun, 1968:53–56; Kelsen, 1968:118, 121–122). A setting with little interaction between its segments may have feuds and fights, but it is not likely to have much law (see Colson, 1953; Nader, 1965:398–399). As a relationship changes over time, however, over days or months or years, its social control changes as well. People completely separate may become acquainted, or today's lovers may draw apart tomorrow, and as this happens law becomes a possibility in their lives (see Starr, 1974:17–19).

Relational distance also predicts and explains the outcomes of legal proceedings. It is less serious, for example, to murder one's wife or friend than to murder a stranger: The penalty is less severe. Thus, in the United States, capital punishment has generally been reserved for crimes occurring between strangers. Judges are reluctant to convict and punish people who hurt their friends and relatives, and the same principle applies to civil matters. All else constant, a plaintiff who sues an intimate is less likely to win than one who sues a stranger. If he wins, he gets less. In a negligence suit, for instance, damages increase with the distance between the victim and the wrongdoer. But people almost never bring negligence suits against their intimates anyway. The same applies to breaches of contract (see Macaulay, 1963:61–65). And it applies to relationships between opposing lawyers as well: The more intimate they are, the more likely is an out-of-court settlement between their clients. When intimates do go to law, what happens depends upon how intimate they are. Among the Lunda of colonial Northern Rhodesia (now Zambia), for example, the tribal courts were reluctant to grant a divorce to anyone, but their reluctance increased with the length of the marriage (Epstein, 1954:6). The same applies to the divorce courts of modern societies. So for a man who kills or beats his wife: The longer they have been married, the less serious is his crime. However it is measured, law decreases at the extremes of intimacy.

It is also possible to measure the distance between a citizen and law itself. The same principle applies: Beyond a point, the closer the relationship between an official and an offender, the less law (see Scheff, 1966:96). Thus, all else constant, a policeman is more lenient toward someone close to him—a relative, friend, neighbor, or fellow policeman. When colonial administrators recruit indigenous people as their policemen, for example, colonial law reflects the structure of indigenous life, with the native authorities lenient toward their intimates, such as fellow kinsmen, but not toward others, such as members of other tribes. In the United States, the government recruited Indians to police Indian reservations, and their severity varied with the strength of their relationships:

As an advance agent of the white man's way he frequently found himself opposed by most of his fellow tribesmen, especially the old, respected leaders. Cast as an informer, a petty police spy, he had to report on the work habits of bands to determine whether they merited sugar, coffee, tobacco, and other rations . . . . The efficiency of the police normally declined as the intimacy of such duties intensified. One official after another reported that his police were reluctant to arrest their friends and relatives, these ties being particularly strong in Indian societies [Hagan, 1966:71, 72].

The same principle applies to officials of every kind. This is why it is an advantage to have a hometown lawyer who knows the judge. Aware of patterns such as this, Italians of the Middle Ages recruited their judges from outside the jurisdictions they were to oversee, and one even prohibited its officials from marrying local women (see Simmel, 1908b:151, 216). In a modern city, by contrast, no one would suggest recruiting officials from outside; hardly anyone knows them anyway.

Modern life amasses people and atomizes social life. Relational distance widens even as people crowd together in time and space, with practically everyone a stranger to everyone else. In fact, since this distance generally increases with population (see Lofland, 1973:8–12), it is possible to predict the quantity of law with the number of people alone: The relationship between law and population is curvilinear (compare Simmel, 1908b: Part 2, Chapter 1; Fortes and Evans-Pritchard, 1940:7–8).

Among precolonial societies such as those of tropical Africa, for example, a state was more likely to appear where population size and density were higher (Stevenson, 1968). Similarly, third-party mediation varies directly with population:

Data were obtained for thirty-nine of the fifty-one societies in the [world] sample on the size of their largest settlement. Societies with mediation have a median largest settlement size of 1000, while those without mediation have a median of 346. Even eliminating the societies with developed cities, the median largest settlement size remains above 500 for societies with mediation [Schwartz and Miller, 1964:165, note 28].

The same applies to other kinds of third-party authority (see Whiting, 1950:91; Firth, 1951:73). And it applies to legislation: As the settlements of early America grew more dense, for instance, new laws of all kinds came into being (see Bacon, 1939:773–777). The appearance of full-time police followed the same principle (Bacon, 1939:779).

Population also predicts the rate at which people go to law for help, and what happens when they do. Thus, up to a point, the larger a community or other setting, the higher is its rate of litigation. Among the Lugbara communities of Uganda, for example, the rate at which people bring each other to court varies directly with population density (Middleton, 1965:48). In India, an industrial dispute in a densely populated community is more likely to be defined as a legal matter, and the larger the firm itself, the more likely this is (Cartwright and Schwartz, 1973:347–350). Where people are more numerous and concentrated, law is, to a point, more severe as well: "Relatively dense societies are more likely to employ harsh sanctions, while lenient controls are found with greater frequency when societies are relatively dispersed [Spitzer, 1975:624]." To a point, then, law increases with urbanization (see Hoebel, 1954:328–329).

Law obeys the rhythm of population, whatever it may be. It may be seasonal in some cases, uneven in others. Bands of nomads may concentrate into larger groups from time to time, for example, such as when the food or water supply improves, and when this happens they may have an episode of law. This was true of the Yahgan of Tierra del Fuego, for instance, a people without law during most of the year:

> The Yahgan, who normally move about in very small groups, unite up to the number of eighty when a beached whale provides food for the participants at an initiation ceremony. Without an election some mature man well posted in traditional usage emerges as the master of ceremonies and henceforth plans the daily routine. What is more, he appoints a constable, who in turn chooses a number of deputies. These policemen exercise genuine legal authority; they forcibly drag refractory tyros to the initiation lodge, overpower a troublemaker, bind him, and let him lie for half a day without food or drink [Lowie, 1948:17–18, citing Gusinde, 1937:199–208, 653, 779ff., 805–961, 1319–1376].

As people distribute and redistribute themselves in time and space, then, their relational distance expands and contracts, and law varies accordingly. This may happen across centuries or decades, or from one day to the next.

* * *

Relational distance also predicts and explains the style of law. For example, it predicts and explains whether law is accusatory, as in the penal and compensatory styles, or remedial, as in the therapeutic and conciliatory styles (see pages 4–5). The conditions of one, in fact, are opposite those of the other: Accusatory law varies directly with relational distance; remedial law varies inversely with relational distance.

Thus, all else constant, strangers are more likely to oppose one another as adversaries, whereas intimates are more likely to offer help (see Lévi-Strauss, 1955:386–387; Gibbs, 1963). This means that in a simple society, where nearly everyone is close to everyone else, law—if present at all—is likely to be more remedial than the law of a more impersonal society. Among the Lozi of Northern Rhodesia (now Zambia), for instance, the *kutas*, or courts, were almost always conciliatory to some degree:

> Most Lozi relationships are multiplex, enduring through the lives of individuals and even generations . . . . Inevitably, therefore, many of the disputes which are investigated by Lozi *kutas* arise not in ephemeral relationships involving single interests, but in relationships which embrace many interests, which depend on similar related relationships, and which may endure into the future . . . . Throughout a court hearing of this kind the judges try to prevent the breaking of relationships, and to make it possible for the parties to live together amicably in the future. Obviously this does not apply to every case, but it is true of a large number, and it is present in some degree in almost all cases. Therefore the court tends to be conciliatory; it strives to effect a compromise acceptable to, and accepted by, all the parties. This is the main task of the judges [Gluckman, 1967:20–21].

As tribal societies modernize, however, communal relationships weaken, and accusatory law increasingly takes hold (see Epstein, 1953:11–12). In Northern Rhodesia, a token of reconciliation may have been enough "to cool one's heart," but now, in Zambia, it increasingly takes punishment (Epstein, 1951:36; 1953:11). The more strangers in a society as a whole, then, the more accusatory and the less remedial is its law (see Gluckman, 1962:443–444). And since courts vary in the kinds of cases they hear—some involving mostly strangers, others mostly intimates—the style of law also varies from court to court within a society (see Gluckman, 1962:443–444; van Velsen, 1969). Even as the intimacy of the parties varies from case to case within a single court, so does the style of law. Society, court, or case, the principle is the same.

RADIAL LOCATION

Just as people may participate more or less in each other's lives, they may participate more or less in social life itself. Some participate fully and usefully; others stay on the margin, hardly involved at all. In this sense, every kind of social life has a center, periphery, and rings of participation (compare Shils, 1961). Every person and group has a location in relation to the center: Each is more or less integrated. This applies to every social function, whether production, reproduction, recreation, or sociability. Some people work; others idle or loiter. Some marry and have children; others stay single. Some are neighborly; others are hermits. In everything, some are more functional than others.

The radial location of a person or group is a status that confers privileges and disabilities. A working man has more of this status than an unemployed man, a mother more than a spinster, the busy more than the indolent, a veteran more than one who did not serve. Radial status may correspond to vertical status, or rank, but this need not be the case (see Barnard, 1946; compare Davis and Moore, 1945). A useful person may be wealthy, but not necessarily, and the same applies to the marginal: Some are central to social life, even essential, and yet low in rank; others who are wealthy do nothing. And a person or group may be central to one social function, marginal to another, integrated here, but not there. The unemployed man may be a good family man; the hard worker may be an old bachelor or recluse. Separately and together, these patterns of participation define the integration of people into social life. And just as a person, family, or organization may be more or less integrated into a community, so a community may be more or less integrated into a society, or a society into a larger group of other societies.

Law varies with its own location in radial space:

Law varies directly with integration.

This means that people in or near the center of social life have more law than those further out. For now, consider only cases in which people are equally integrated, whether poorly or well, since cases pertaining to people who are not equally integrated have peculiarities of their own (see next section).

All else constant, an offense between two employed men is more likely to result in legal action than an offense between two who are unemployed, one between two socialites more than one between two isolates, one between two residents more than one between two transients. If a vagrant victimizes another vagrant, for instance, the police are less likely to hear about it. If they are summoned, the police are less likely to make an arrest, and, if they do, a prosecutor, judge, or jury is less likely to be severe. In other words, an offense between marginal people is less serious than an offense between people more integrated into social life.

Lawsuits of every kind—negligence, defamation, inheritance, or whatever—all are less likely among marginal people. The lawsuits of the marginal are less successful as well. Even if a marginal man wins a case from another equally low in radial status, he is less likely to be compensated as much as someone more integrated would be: His wellbeing is not worth so much, whether what is involved is his person, reputation, or finances. But then much of law regulates matters relevant only to more integrated people anyway, such as employment, exchange, the conduct of organizations, government, and marriage. Marginal groups also have less law among themselves. If social life is concentric, then, with rings of participation, the distribution of law is conical, with ever more toward the center.

RADIAL DIRECTION

Even if social life is concentric, this does not mean that people interact only with others of their own radial status. In the case of crime or other deviant behavior, for instance, integrated people may victimize marginal people, or vice versa. Hence, it is possible to describe deviant behavior with the radial location of the people it implicates. It may be confined to the center of social life, to the periphery, or to somewhere between. Or it may have a direction in radial space, with the deviant more or less integrated than his victim. Centrifugal deviance offends outwardly, with the deviant more integrated than his victim, whereas centripetal deviance offends inwardly. In each case, the direction of law is opposite that of the deviant behavior, with centrifugal law defining and responding to centripetal deviance, and centripetal law to centrifugal deviance. Moreover, the quantity of law varies accordingly:

Centrifugal law is greater than centripetal law.

This means that the offense of a marginal person or group against an integrated person or group is more serious than an offense in the opposite direction. For example, if the victim is an employed man, married, a father, and otherwise an active participant in his community, but the offender is a lone transient with no visible means of support, this is more serious than if the same offense occurs in the opposite direction, with a transient the victim of a well-integrated member of the community. The same principle applies to civil as well as criminal matters, and to every stage of the legal process.

Integration is a matter of degree, however, and the difference between people in this respect—the radial distance between them—also predicts and explains the quantity of law. Centrifugal law increases with this distance, whereas centripetal law decreases:

Centrifugal law varies directly with radial distance.

But:

Centripetal law varies inversely with radial distance.

Thus, the likelihood of a complaint by an integrated person against a marginal person increases with the difference in integration between them, as does the likelihood that the complaint will succeed. But the likelihood of a complaint in the opposite direction, from a marginal person against someone more integrated, decreases as the difference between them increases, and the same applies to the success of the complaint. It follows that, all else constant—including the radial status of the offender—law varies directly with the integration of the victim. And, all else constant—including the status of the victim—law varies inversely with the integration of the offender. First consider the offender.

A crime by an unemployed man is more serious than a crime by an employed man. It is still more serious if an unemployed offender has no family, and yet more so if he is a transient, unknown in the community. It is ever less serious, however, if an employed offender has a good work record, a large family, and is known for his service to the community. In every way, a marginal man is more vulnerable to law; by comparison, an integrated man has an immunity. A marginal man is more likely to have a lawsuit brought against him, for example, more likely to have the police called against him, to be stopped and questioned by the police, to be arrested, prosecuted, or to lose his case, to have heavy damages demanded of him, or to be severely punished. His bail is higher, he is less likely to be placed on probation or otherwise diverted from punishment, less likely to appeal his case, to win a reversal if he does appeal, or to be released on parole. Among women, a mother is treated more leniently than a woman without children. Among young people who do not work, a student is more likely to be given another chance, and all the more if he participates in athletics or other school activities.

Marginality itself may even be defined as illegal. For example, with the breakdown of feudal society in the late Middle Ages, large numbers of serfs wandered from their ancestral homes to forage and beg across Europe, and, as this happened, antivagrancy law appeared and spread throughout the Continent (see Marx, 1890: Chapter 28; Chambliss, 1964). In England, for instance, a law of 1530 condemned "sturdy vagabonds" to be

> tied to the cart-tail and whipped until the blood streams from their bodies, then to swear an oath to go back to their birthplace or to where they have lived the last three years and to put themselves to labor [Marx, 1890:734].

A law of 1547 held that if a vagabond idled about for three days he was to be returned to his birthplace, branded with a redhot iron with the letter V on the breast and be set to work, in chains, in the streets or at some other labor. If the vagabond gives a false birthplace, he is then to become the slave for life of this place, of its inhabitants, or its corporation, and to be branded with an S [Marx, 1890:735].

Repeat offenders were subject to execution as felons (Marx, 1890:735–736). Late eighteenth- and early nineteenth-century French vagrants were subject to considerable control as well, and they were easy to recognize, since common people were required to wear metal badges identifying their occupations (Cobb, 1970:24–25). Early New York City commissioned "vagabond and stranger police" to watch over people of this kind (Bacon, 1939:781). In early twentieth-century America, large numbers of men and boys moved from place to place with the seasons, working as farm laborers during the warmer months and surviving however else they could during the winter. Known as "tramps" or "hobos," they were everywhere subject to special attention from the police:

Whether a major offender or not, the fact is that the homeless man is almost always liable to arrest as a vagrant. He is marked as a potential offender. He always faces the possibility of being arrested on suspicion. Where the ex-convict is harassed by the authorities because they have his record, the tramp is often held because they do not have his record. Often migrants are taken from freight trains and transported many miles to the scenes of some offense only to be turned loose. Often they are held for days in local jails until they can prove an alibi or their identity can be established. For them there is no redress [Anderson, 1923:165].

In modern America, vagrants still are more vulnerable (see, e.g., Spradley, 1970: Chapters 4–5; Wiseman, 1970:90). And the same principle explains modern Russia's "antiparasite laws," designed to eliminate "persons avoiding socially useful work [quoted in Berman, 1963:291; see also his pages 292–298]."

Also vulnerable to law is social withdrawal of every kind. This explains the punishment of someone who deserts his family or army, and it explains the prohibition of suicide. To be unmarried may be subject to suspicion as well. Thus, in colonial New England, a single person was not permitted to live alone or with other single people but had to live with a family (see, e.g., Haskins, 1960:80; Demos, 1970a:78). If in trouble with the law, he risked greater punishment. The single are also subject to more law in modern societies (see, e.g., Sutherland and Cressey, 1960:186). And illegitimate children have disabilities in some societies (see Montesquieu, 1748: Section 6), as do others with marginal origins, such as the children of suicides, and orphans of other kinds. To grow up in a family supported by charity is a kind of marginality as well. On the other hand, those with origins in the center of social life, such as the children of early settlers or old families, are subject to less law. In Imperial Rome, this applied to veterans and their children (Garnsey, 1968:5). A record of service is an advantage everywhere: The integration of a person, like other kinds of status, is known not only by what he is today but by his history, including all he has ever done.

Now hold constant the offender, and law varies directly with the integration of his victim. In Laos, for instance, where a murderer may pay a "head price" in place of a long prison term, the price varies directly with the social importance of the victim:

> When homicide comes to the attention of the central government authorities, the suspected murderer is jailed. Then a hearing occurs before a government official. If the suspect is declared guilty, then a *khaa hua* (head price) is set. The head price varies according to the age and social status of the victim, whether he was married or had children. If the head price is paid to the victim's survivors, the murderer may be in prison for a few months to a few years. If it is not paid, he will spend ten to twenty years in prison [Westermeyer, 1971:566].

In every legal system, the cost of illegality increases with the integration of the person who is offended—as known by his contribution to the life of the community, the length of time he has been a resident, the size of his family, even his gregariousness. The closer to the center he is, the more likely is law to be invoked on his behalf, the more quickly do the police or other authorities respond, the more extensive is an investigation of his problem, the speedier is the trial. An integrated citizen is more likely to win his lawsuit and to win compensation,and more of it,or whatever else he demands. All of this applies in proportion to his integration and the marginality of his opponent.

* * *

Deviant behavior by a marginal person or group against an integrated person or group, or centripetal deviance, is the most serious, followed by deviant behavior between integrated people, then between marginal people, and lastly deviant behavior by an integrated person or group against a marginal person or group, or centrifugal deviance. In other words, law of every kind—from complaints to punishments or damages—decreases in this order. This applies, however, only when all else is constant. When the radial direction of deviant behavior is the same across the cases in a comparison, for example, the integration of the parties may vary, and so law may vary accordingly (see pages 48, 50). In other ways as well, two or more principles may apply at once, sometimes consistent with each other, sometimes at odds. Together, these predict and explain the quantity and style of law.

MARGINALITY AND DEVIANT BEHAVIOR

One theory of deviant behavior holds that a person who is poorly integrated, or marginal, is more motivated to deviate. For example, one version of this theory explains the motivation to commit suicide with social isolation, such as a lack of family or religious life (Durkheim, 1897: Book 2, Chapters 2–3). Another explains conversion to a radical sect as, in part, a response to social disintegration, such as the end of a marriage or career (Lofland and Stark, 1965:870). Another explains juvenile delinquency with a lack of attachments to parents, school, and peers (Hirschi, 1969). The unmarried, divorced, or unemployed, the truant, migrant, or friendless, and the product of a broken home—all, according to marginality theory, have a greater motivation to engage in deviant behavior.

In fact, marginal people are disproportionately subject to law, and so, in this sense, they are more deviant than other people. In the United States, for example, the rate of commitment to prisons and reformatories is higher for single and divorced people than for those who are married or widowed (Sutherland and Cressey, 1960:186). The same is true of other societies and of other aspects of the criminal process (see Sutherland and Cressey, 1960:187). Similarly, truants in the United States have a higher rate of juvenile delinquency than those who attend school regularly (Shaw and McKay, 1969: Chapter 5). Marginality theory predicts these facts, explaining them with the greater deviant motivation of the person who is poorly integrated. Note, however, that the theory of law predicts and explains the same facts.

At every stage of the legal process, a marginal person is more vulnerable to law. Since law varies inversely with the integration of the offender (see pages 50–51), so do criminality and delinquency. All else constant, then, a person without work, a family, or other involvements is more likely to get into trouble with the law. Indeed, the authorities may even justify their severity by invoking the marginality theory of deviant behavior (see Cicourel, 1968:97–102). This does not mean that the conduct of marginal and integrated people is always the same. But no matter what it is, the conduct of marginal people is more likely to be defined as criminal or delinquent in the first place. Thus, although the theory of law predicts the same facts as the marginality theory of deviant behavior, each has a different explanation.

THE BEHAVIOR OF SOCIAL CONTROL

Social control in general may be explained by the distribution of people in relation to each other, including their differentiation, intimacy, and integration. Hence, morphological variables that explain law also explain social control in societies without law. Among the Nuer of the Sudan, for instance, a man traditionally paid compensation for homicide only if the victim was more distant than a close kinsman, but not so distant as a total stranger:

> The killing of a stranger, especially of a foreigner, who does not come within the most expanded form of the social structure, is not really wrong (*duer*) at all . . . . The killing of a fellow tribesman, and to a much lesser extent a fellow Nuer of another tribe who is within the orbit of the killer's social sphere, is a wrong because it is an offense against the stability of society in its most extended form. But it is a private delict and not a crime, and demands only retaliation or restitution. The closer the relationship between the component tribal segments involved, the greater the sanction for restitu-

tion . . . . Finally in the narrowest definition of blood-relationship, where kinship is a reality and not merely a fictional social form—that is, within the lineage or the extended family group—restitution becomes less and less necessary because the persons who assist in the payment of compensation are also the recipients. [Thus,] a man does not pay compensation at all if he kills his own wife—a rare occurrence—for he would have to pay it to himself [Howell, 1954:207–208, 57–58; see also Scott, 1976].

Similarly, among the camel-herding Bedouin of Cyrenaica, traditionally a man paid no compensation to a near kinsman:

Corporate identity [in the smallest genealogical unit] is conceptualized as "one bone" or "one body" . . . . In Bedouin thinking, an injury to "the one body" is an injury to all its parts. Blood-money payments by members of a corporation to one or more of its members is a contradiction in terms. In the same way vengeance is also excluded, for this merely doubles the original loss [Peters, 1967:263].

In societies with law, intimacy also explains social control of other kinds. Thus, everywhere, conduct otherwise defined as deviant is more likely to be accepted, or "normalized," when it occurs between intimates:

Normalization is readily perceived in family interaction where a wide variety of idiosyncratic behavior becomes acceptable . . . . A great deal of behavior which in another context would be defined as "delinquent" is normalized because the rules of interaction are different. Even more impressive is the normalization of behavior which, when projected against the diagnostic criteria of formal psychiatry, would be looked upon as "neurotic" or "psychotic" [Lemert, 1964:86].

Now, in more detail, consider how morphological variables predict and explain the social control of witchcraft.

In societies where witches are named, the accusation typically follows a misfortune such as an illness or accident. The witch may be subject to legal action, as in Renaissance Europe or seventeenth-century America, but in many societies this is not a governmental matter. In fact, the naming of witches is less likely to be found in a society where law is highly developed (Whiting, 1950:85–90; Fritz, 1971; see also Swanson, 1960: Chapter 8). In any case, not everyone is equally vulnerable to an accusation of witchcraft. And whether legal or not, the naming of witches obeys the same principles. For example, an intimate, such as a parent, child, or spouse, is less likely to be named as a witch than someone more distant from the accuser, such as an in-law, neighbor, or other acquaintance. But someone extremely distant, a total stranger, is also less likely to be named. This was true, for instance, among the Azande of the Sudan (Evans-Pritchard, 1937:31–32, 104–106), the Cewa of Zambia (Marwick, 1965:177–178, 187), the Nyakyusa of Tanzania (Wilson, 1951a:102–103), the Pondo of South Africa (Wilson, 1951b), the Navajo of the American Southwest (Kluckhohn, 1944:104–106), and various Oceanian tribes (Marwick, 1964). This also applied to the witchcraft prosecutions in Tudor and Stuart England (Macfarlane, 1970: Chapter 12; Thomas, 1970:59–62, 66; 1971:546–560) and colonial America (Demos, 1970b:1315–1319). Whether law is involved or not, then, the relationship between the naming of witches and relational distance is curvilinear.

Especially in simpler societies, relational distance tends to increase with the distance between people in time and space, or physical distance. A witch is therefore likely to live some distance from his or her victim, but not very far away either. Among the Zapotec Indians of Mexico, for example, a witch is likely to live on the other side of his accuser's village, or in the next village, about five miles away:

> An illness or sudden reversal of fortune initiates a search procedure among those who could have bewitched you . . . . One operates from within his circle of kinsmen and reaches out through them to the rest of the village, attempting to impose his identification on others [Selby, 1974:119–120].

Hence, each person or family finds its witches in a different location in time and space:

> The family I lived with pointed out that, although there were some witches around the house where I was living . . . , most of the witches in the village did not live around our house—in the upper part of the village—but rather in the lower part. Fortunately, I had a very good informant who lived in the middle of the lower part, and I approached him carefully and discreetly in the hope that he would be of help in identifying the witches, whom I hoped subsequently to interview. He was. He pointed out that, although there were one or two witches in the lower part of the village, most of the witches lived in the upper part . . . . The majority of local witches who are not from the local community come from the neighboring town, where the population is rife with witches [Selby, 1974:119, 124].

On the other hand, the Zapotec do not accuse people who live still further away, beyond a day's journey (see Selby, 1974:119–128). In fact, many tribes hold that witchcraft does not even work over a long distance (e.g., Evans-Pritchard, 1937:36–37; Wilson, 1951a:102–103).

An accusation of witchcraft is also less likely among people with little or no division of labor, and, at the other extreme, among those who depend upon each other to the point of symbiosis. Between these extremes, an accusation is more likely among people with a degree of differentiation, but not so much as among those with a developed system of law. It is less likely among hunters, gatherers, or herdsmen, for example, but also in a modern city (see Baxter, 1972:177, 184; Douglas, 1973: Chapter 7). Over time, then, the naming of witches increases as a simple society differentiates, but only to a point, after which it declines and disappears (see Mitchell, 1965; Swartz, 1969; Marwick, 1970). In short, the relationship between the naming of witches and differentiation is curvilinear.

Finally, consider the radial location and direction of social control. People in or near the center of social life have more social control than those on the margin: Social control varies directly with integration. But from the center outward, toward less integrated people, it is greater than from the margin inward, toward more integrated people. Hence, although the naming of witches is more likely near the center of social life than on the periphery, an accusation against a marginal by a more integrated person is more likely than the reverse. In Tudor and Stuart England, for example, the accused was most likely to be an old woman who lived alone and was not a productive member of her community:

> Witches were . . . often women and especially widows, whose means of subsistence were often inadequate without neighborly support. The position of such people had been weakened by the decline of customary manorial arrangements for the support of the elderly . . . . Many were dependent upon their neighbors, while lacking the institutional recognition afforded those in receipt of poor relief [Thomas, 1970:64].

The most vulnerable woman was a kind of vagrant in her own village, someone who occasionally begged food, drink, or other help from her neighbors. When misfortune struck someone who had turned her away, she was the first to be blamed (Thomas, 1970:62).

As the traditional family weakened across Europe—but before a new social order had taken hold—more and more of these marginal women appeared. More than ever before appeared in the sixteenth and seventeenth centuries, the time of the great witch hunts:

> Here for the first time in European history was a large group of women who remained spinsters. Their numbers were of course augmented by widows, who often formed 10–20 per cent of the tax-paying population . . . . The growing number of unmarried women would have appeared as a seditious element in society, especially after the death of their fathers removed them from patriarchal control altogether. Until society learned to adjust to the new family patterns, one could argue that unmarried women would have been especially susceptible to attack. This conclusion would support the commonplace observation that widows and spinsters were the most commonly accused of witchcraft, far out of proportion to their numbers in society [Midelfort, 1972:184–185].

Among the Navajo Indians as well, an unproductive old person was more likely to be named as a witch, and so was a childless woman (Kluckhohn, 1944:104). And, everywhere, an isolate is also more vulnerable to these accusations. Among the Paiute Indians of Oregon, for instance, a person with few close relatives or friends was more vulnerable (Whiting, 1950:64–65). Among the Nyakyusa, it was the person who was not sociable:

> The type most usually described as a witch is the person whose character makes him (or her) to some extent isolated and unpopular—a proud man who treats his neighbors with disdain; a retiring man who always keeps silent in public; a glum wife, or one who fails to greet the other women she meets and to inquire after their children. Such people are treated by their neighbors with less courtesy and hospitality than the traditional ideals of good manners demand. "Perhaps we do not summon him to drink beer, or to eat with us: and then when our cows fail to give milk we think, 'doubtless it is he who is throttling them' " [Wilson, 1951a:104].

Whatever goes wrong anywhere, those who are marginal to social life are more likely to be blamed. In general, their conduct is more likely to be defined as deviant, and whatever they do is more serious.

4

CULTURE

Culture is the symbolic aspect of social life, including expressions of what is true, good, and beautiful (see Parsons, 1951:57–58; Parsons, Shils, Allport, Kluckhohn, Murray, Sears, Sheldon, Stouffer, and Tolman, 1951:5, 21). It thus includes ideas about the nature of reality, whether theoretical or practical, and whether supernatural, metaphysical, or empirical. Examples are science, technology, religion, magic, and folklore. It also includes conceptions of what ought to be, what is right and wrong, proper and improper—apart from the behavior of social control itself. Values, ideology, morality, and law have a symbolic aspect of this kind. And, finally, culture includes aesthetic life of all sorts, the fine arts and the popular, such as poetry and painting, clothing and other decorative art, architecture, and even the culinary arts. It should be clear that culture has an existence of its own, apart from the way people experience it. It appears in every social setting, and it varies in quantity and style from one place and time to the next. In other words, culture behaves (see White, 1949:xviii; 1975:20). It is possible to predict and explain the behavior of culture of every kind.

It is also possible to explain other social life with culture, and one aspect of culture with another. An example of this strategy is the theory of historical idealism, which understands social life as an expression of a unique cultural spirit that works itself into social action over time, the ideal ever becoming the real (see Hegel, e.g., 1821:122–223). Similarly, many interpretations of stable societies, such as tribal societies, view everyday life as an embodiment of one or more cultural themes (e.g., Benedict, 1934). Another example is the theory of integralism, which relates every aspect of culture to every other, all shifting together over time with the fluctuation of more basic cultural values (Sorokin, 1937). Still another is the theory of institutionalization, according to which cultural values guide social action toward an equilibrium under changing historical conditions (Parsons and Shils, 1951:190–204; see also Mayhew, 1968: Chapter 1).

Cultural theories have been applied to law as well. For instance, the theory of historical jurisprudence understands law as an expression of its larger cultural setting, unique to each society and time (e.g., Savigny, 1814). Another explains law with "public opinion" and the "spirit of the age" (Dicey, 1905:462–463). Some explain it with custom (e.g., Sumner, 1906; Lévy-Bruhl, 1951; Bohannan, 1965:34–37; 1968), others with cultural values (e.g., Sorokin, 1937: Volume 2, Part 2; Gibbs, 1962; see also Gusfield, 1963), still others with intellectual as well as normative aspects of culture (e.g., Hoebel, 1954:13–16; Smith and Roberts, 1954; Hoebel, 1965; 1970; see also Mayhew, 1968: Chapter 1). It should be noted that law has cultural aspects of its own, its own images of reality and its own ideology, values, and rules of every sort. This includes arguments and testimony from one case to the next. There are innumerable studies of modern legal culture, including much of the scholarship of lawyers themselves. Studies of tribal and other kinds of traditional legal culture also are available (e.g., Haar, 1939; Schapera, 1955; Gluckman, 1965). It is possible to explain law—as social control—with the culture of law (see, e.g., Selznick, 1961; 1969). More generally, it is possible to explain law with the quantity of culture of all kinds, its diversity, and the cultural location and direction of law itself.

THE QUANTITY OF CULTURE

Culture varies in its quantity from one setting to another. In some places it is so rich that a newcomer needs months or years to learn its many features, or he never does; others have only a few shreds of culture, readily known by anyone. Some societies have more culture than others, some groups, situations, or individuals more than others. There is variation in the number of languages, concepts, and ideas, in the volume of folklore and science, of religion and magic, values and customs, clothing and other decoration. Every place and person displays culture of many kinds, but some more than others. And, over time, culture increases and decreases. In short, it is possible to count every kind of culture, or all of it together. Compare a modern to a tribal society, a scientific laboratory to a bus station, a professor to his children.

Where culture is sparse, so is law; where it is rich, law flourishes. The more culture, the more law:

Law varies directly with culture.

Across societies, the least culture is found among tribal people, especially hunters and gatherers who live as nomads. Examples are the Bushmen of South Africa, the Pygmies of Zaire, and the Negritos of the Philippines. People such as these have only one language, one religion, one theory of anything. In comparison to a modern society, they have few ideas, values, or arts. Within a single band or tribe, all of the dwellings are alike. They have little furniture, and it is alike from one dwelling to the next. The same applies to clothing: The men dress alike, as do the women, and what they wear is the same from day to day. Jewelry, hairstyles, and cosmetics are the same. Song and dance are the same, changing little from year to year. Even the food is much the same from day to day, meal to meal. In its everyday life, a society of this kind has no law.

On the other hand, if a society is literate, if it has many subcultures, beliefs, monuments or large buildings, an elaborate technology for the production of food or anything else, if it has science in the modern sense, it has law. And if this symbolic life grows over time, so does law. Hence, in the short term, legislation and litigation increase during periods of creativity or other kinds of cultural effervescence. In Europe, for instance, law grew especially fast during the Renaissance, during the late eighteenth and early nineteenth centuries, and the late nineteenth and early twentieth centuries. Over a longer term, as culture reaches the scale seen in large modern societies such as the Soviet Union and the United States, law reaches further and further into the life of the people. The culture of law itself develops to such a degree that entire schools are devoted to its study.

The quantity of culture varies across a single society as well. Some regions may have more than others, for instance, with coastal regions typically having more culture than interior regions, urban areas more than rural, valleys and plateaus more than slopes. Some communities have more than others, some neighborhoods, occupations, organizations, or families have more than others. All else constant, wherever symbolic life is most advanced, so is law. In a single society or community, then, law is unevenly distributed across cultural space. Similarly, some individuals have more culture than others. Again, this is a question of quantity, not quality, a question of cultural status in an objective, not a subjective, sense. An individual's culture depends upon how many ideas he has, what he wears, eats, makes, watches, and plays. And the quantity of culture in his life predicts the quantity of law in his life. Among themselves, people with more cultural status are more litigious than others. If a cultured person—in this quantitative sense—offends another cultured person, law is more severe than when an uncultured person offends another like himself. In other words, matters between more cultured people are more serious. Accordingly, law varies directly with literacy and education. Literate and educated people are more likely to bring lawsuits against others, for instance, and they are more likely to win, and to win more. However each is measured, law varies directly with culture.

This even applies to the culture of law itself. As social control, law varies directly with its own culture, the quantity of its doctrines and rules. Where legal culture is richer, legal control is greater: Litigation is more likely, damages are heavier, sentences longer. This pattern appears across societies and across history, across areas of law, courts, and cases. Wherever it is possible to compare the quantity of culture of any kind, it is possible to predict and explain the quantity of law.

CULTURAL DIRECTION: TYPE I

Just as deviant behavior may have vertical direction, upward or downward between ranks (see page 21), or radial direction, inward or outward from the center of social life (see pages 49–50), so it may have cultural direction, between different quantities of culture (see also page 69). An offense by an uneducated person against an educated person, for example, is a deviant act from less to more culture. In this case, the direction of law is the opposite, from more to less culture, the same as the direction of a complaint. Cultural direction of this kind predicts and explains the quantity of law:

Law is greater in a direction toward
less culture than toward more culture.

Thus, all else constant, an offense by someone with less culture than his victim is more serious than an offense in the opposite direction. If the offense is toward more culture, such as an offense against someone with more education than the offender, law of every kind is greater: A call to the police is more likely, as is a complaint, lawsuit, conviction, severe sentence, heavy damages, or whatever. In a dispute between groups as well, the party with higher cultural status is more likely to complain to a legal agency, and its complaint is more likely to succeed in every way.

Moreover, the magnitude of a difference in culture, or the cultural distance, also predicts and explains the quantity of law. But this depends upon the direction of law in cultural space:

In a direction toward less culture, law
varies directly with cultural distance.

But:

> *In a direction toward more culture, law*
> *varies inversely with cultural distance.*

Thus, if an offender is less educated than his victim, the seriousness of the offense increases with the difference in education between them. But if an offender is more educated than his victim, the seriousness of the offense decreases as this difference increases. An implication is that, all else constant—including the victim's characteristics—law varies inversely with the culture of the offender. Correlatively, all else constant—including the offender's characteristics—law varies directly with the culture of the victim.

First consider the advantage of cultured offenders. In fourteenth-century England, for instance, the doctrine called "benefit of clergy," originally a privilege by which a clergyman charged with a felony generally was subject only to ecclesiastical authority, was applied to any man who could read a verse in the Bible (Stephen, 1883:461; Pollock and Maitland, 1898: Volume 1, 445). After 1487, however, this privilege could be invoked only once by a layman, at which time he was branded on the thumb for future identification:

> Till 1487 any one who knew how to read might commit murder as often as he pleased, with no other result than that of being delivered to the ordinary [ecclesiastical authority] to make his purgation . . . . That this should have been the law for several centuries seems hardly credible, but there is no doubt that it was. Even after 1487 a man who could read could commit murder once with no other punishment than that of having M branded on the brawn of his left thumb [Stephen, 1883:463–464].

A literate layman was not so privileged as a clergyman, then, though typically he was not so cultured either. But he was better off than an illiterate, the least cultured of all. The same applies in other societies as well: Wherever some are literate and others not, literacy is a legal advantage. So is education: All else constant, the more educated an offender, the less serious is his offense. In a modern society, for example, those with a university education are the least vulnerable to law, followed by those with a high school education, and lastly by those with only a grammar school education or less.

On the other hand, the more educated the victim of an offense, the more serious it is. Whoever may be a repository of culture— whether a teacher, professional, priest, or shaman—receives more protection from law. A crime against him is worse, and, in general, he is more easily offended. He is more likely to complain to the authorities, to take his case to court, and to get what he wants. In modern America, for example, the more educated victim of an automobile accident is more likely to hire a lawyer (Conard *et al.*, 1964:226–227). In matters of all kinds, a more educated person is more likely to seek the services of a lawyer (see Mayhew and Reiss, 1969:310, 314). He is also more likely to take his case to court.

* * *

The most serious kind of deviant behavior is an offense from less to more culture, followed by an offense between people equally cultured, then by an offense between people equally uncultured, and finally by an offense from more to less culture. An offense by an illiterate against a university graduate is more serious than an offense between university graduates, for instance, followed by an offense between illiterates and, lastly, an offense by a university graduate against an illiterate. But this applies only insofar as other variables are constant, including other variable aspects of culture.

CULTURAL LOCATION

Some kinds of culture are more conventional than others: They happen more frequently. Some ideas appear more frequently, for example, and the same applies to religions, clothing, foods, dances, theories, hair styles, moralities, medicines, or games. In some societies nearly everyone is the same; other societies have subcultures and much individuality. Some people follow the most common patterns of their society in practically everything they do; others are eccentric, with many peculiarities. In short, conventionality is a quantitative variable. In modern America, for instance, a bourgeois style of life is more conventional than a bohemian style—simply because it is more frequent. A Protestant or Catholic is more conventional than a Jew—simply because there are more Protestants and Catholics. An Italian or Irishman is more conventional than a Greek or Armenian. A Democrat or Republican is more conventional than a Communist. A tobacco or alcohol habit is more conventional than a heroin or cocaine habit. Finally, it should be clear that conventionality defines a kind of cultural status, with some people having more than others.

Just as law varies with rank, or its vertical location (see pages 16–21), and integration, or its radial location (see pages 48–49), so for conventionality, or its cultural location. Law increases as it nears the mainstream of culture, decreasing as it moves away:

Law varies directly with conventionality.

For these purposes, consider only people equal in cultural status, since law also varies with its direction from one cultural status to another (see next section). Among themselves, then, conventional people have more law than unconventional people.

All else constant, an American bourgeois is more likely to bring a lawsuit against a fellow bourgeois than a bohemian against a fellow bohemian. Similarly, a Presbyterian is more likely to bring a lawsuit against a fellow Presbyterian than is a Mormon or Jehovah's Witness to bring a lawsuit against a fellow Mormon or Jehovah's Witness. Subcultures of all kinds have less law. Thus, in the United States, there is little law in Chinatowns, Greektowns, Little Italies, on Indian reservations, and in ethnic enclaves of other kinds. There is also little within millenarian and other unconventional religions, among political radicals and other utopians, among mystics, pacifists, vegetarians, nudists, tourists, and motorcyclists. And, among these, law is least likely among the least conventional. This applies everywhere, and to every kind of law. But now consider the behavior of law when one party is more conventional than another.

CULTURAL DIRECTION: TYPE II

Just as deviant behavior may have a direction between different quantities of culture, such as between people with different levels of education (see page 65), so it may have a direction between different degrees of conventionality, such as, in America, between a bourgeois and a bohemian or a gentile and a Jew. Cultural direction of this kind involves a difference in the frequency of culture, regardless of its quantity in an absolute sense. In such cases the direction of law is opposite that of the deviant behavior, whether from more to less conventionality, or from less to more. Moreover, this predicts and explains the quantity of law:

> *Law is greater in a direction toward less*
> *conventionality than toward more conventionality.*

In other words, an offense by an unconventional against a conventional person or group is more serious than an offense in the opposite direction, with the offender more conventional than the victim.

In nineteenth-century America, for example, a crime by an Indian against a white was more serious than the reverse:

It will be seen at once . . . that the United States was determined to provide an adequate judicial system for the Indian Country and that the Indians were to be treated with equally scrupulous justice as the whites. In practice, however, there were serious discrepancies . . . . Against Indian criminals [the laws] were invoked again and again. If an Indian committed a crime against a white—and murder was the offense foremost in mind—the criminal was demanded from the tribe by the United States . . . . If the accused Indian was not delivered up, a military expedition was sent to apprehend him or hostages were seized and held until the criminal appeared . . . . However reluctant the Indian tribes might have been to turn over their members to the United States for punishment, they had a remarkably good record in doing so . . . .

> Crimes against the Indians, on the other hand, were so numerous and widespread that their control by judicial means proved impossible . . . . The frequency of offenses committed against Indians by the frontier whites—among which outright murder was commonplace—was shocking . . . . The murders and other aggressions of the whites against the Indians provided one of the great sources of friction between the two races . . . . The laws and treaties were not effective in themselves, and the lack of enforcement made a mockery of the statutes. The typical frontier community could not be brought to convict a man who injured or murdered an Indian [Prucha, 1962:193–194, 198, 199].

American Indians still have a disadvantage, but it is not so great as it once was. Neither is the difference in conventionality between Indians and whites—a cultural distance—so great as before. Law varies with cultural distance of this kind, depending upon the direction of law in cultural space:

> *In a direction toward less conventionality,*
> *law varies directly with cultural distance.*

But:

> *In a direction toward more conventionality,*
> *law varies inversely with cultural distance.*

Accordingly, the closer Indians and whites become, the more equal will be the quantity of law flowing between them in each direction. Two general implications follow from these propositions. First: All else constant—including the victim's characteristics—law varies inversely with the conventionality of the offender. And second: All else constant—including the offender's characteristics—law varies directly with the conventionality of the victim. Since Indians in the United States are still a cultural minority, then, it is understandable that they receive more severe sentences than whites (see Hall and Simkus, 1975). An Indian is also more vulnerable to a criminal complaint, arrest, prosecution, or conviction, and to civil proceedings of all kinds. If an Indian is a victim, however, the offense is not so serious.

  Colonial and other premodern societies often combine different ethnic groups into single administrative units, making it possible to observe how the legal fate of each group varies with the relative frequency of its cultural patterns. In colonial Tanganyika (now Tanzania), for instance, the Kaguru Native Authority (now Ukaguru) included five different tribes: Kaguru, Ngulu, Kamba, Gogo, and Baraguyu. Some were patrilineal and pastoral, others matrilineal and sedentary, some Nilo-Hamitic, others Bantu (see Beidelman, 1966:120). The great majority, however, were Kaguru, a Bantu people, and so were the legal officials. It is therefore understandable that the Kaguru judges were harsher toward non-Kaguru, especially the Baraguyu, who were the most unconventional people in the district (Beidelman, 1967:34). Even in marital disputes, if one spouse was Kaguru and the other not, the court's decision invariably favored the Kaguru's side (Beidelman, 1967:32). In the Musoma region of the same colony, where Masai were few in number, "cattle theft by the Masai was reported to the police, but . . . far more frequent and economically damaging thefts within the district and its communities were rarely reported [Tanner, 1966:3]." These patterns persist in independent Tanzania, but increasingly the major difference is between the moderns and those who remain traditional in their life style. Thus, in Ukaguru, the Baraguyu cling to the past more than any, and so they are still the most vulnerable to law (Beidelman, 1967:42–43).

In modern America, a person who is bohemian in his life style is more vulnerable to law. For instance, a customer in a department store is more likely to report a bohemian shoplifter—one with a "hippie" appearance—than a conventional shoplifter (Steffensmeier and Terry, 1973:425). The same pattern repeats itself at every stage of the criminal process, with the store manager more likely to call the police about a bohemian, the police more likely to arrest him, the prosecutor more likely to prosecute him, and the judge more likely to convict him and to impose a severe punishment. Any person who is unconventional in his dress, speech, manner, ideas, or anything else, is more vulnerable to law of every kind. In a community of churchgoers, the nonbeliever is more vulnerable. A boy who does not go to Sunday school is more likely to get into trouble. In general, the more a person resembles his neighbors, the more he blends into the crowd, the more immunity from law he enjoys.

Unconventionality itself is more vulnerable to law. For example, after the conquest of the Plains Indian, the American government discouraged various folkways and ceremonies among the Indians, such as the sun dance, the scalp dance, traditional Indian dress, and braided hair (see Hagan, 1966:70, 84, 107–108, 122). On some reservations, however, Indian officials punished unconventionality from an Indian standpoint. For instance, Pueblo officials punished Americanization among Indian children:

> Boys and girls who refused to take off their [American] dress have been forcibly stripped of their clothing, tied to a stake, and whipped. Parents who refused to make their children put on Indian dress have been tied by thumbs, hung to posts, and flogged. Those who wanted to send their children to school have been subjected to a like indignity [Hoebel, 1969:94, quoting letter from W. P. McClure, Indian Agent, to Commissioner of Indian Affairs, September 2, 1889; punctuation edited].

The same pattern is illustrated by the prohibition of ostentatious clothing among the Puritans of colonial Massachusetts (see Haskins, 1960:77). During their early years the Puritans entirely excluded unconventional people from their communities:

> To secure the enclave of common believers that it sought, a town did not simply deny inhabitancy to outlanders. It looked carefully into every man who approached its borders, English and American as well as alien, and its disapproval meant that he moved elsewhere. For a man did not simply move into a town in eighteenth-century Massachusetts: he applied for admission. Each community retained the right to accept only those that it wished, and that right persisted without challenge to the time of the Revolution. "Such whose dispositions do not suit us, whose society will be hurtful to us," were simply refused entry as enemies of harmony and homogeneity . . . . They could not even be entertained by inhabitants unless such inhabitants obtained the permission of the town [Zuckerman, 1970:111].

Modern societies such as the United States also restrict immigration across their borders, with those whose culture is least represented in the existing population generally having the most difficulty gaining admission.

People may also be punished for their unconventional ideas. An example seen in many societies is the punishment of heresy (e.g., Pike, 1876:49–65; Sangar, 1967:172–174). People with unpopular political opinions may also be subject to law. A less direct strategy is the prosecution of unconventional people as witches (see, e.g., Cohn, 1975). And, beyond measures such as these, an entire subculture may be prohibited. In seventeenth-century France, for example, Louis XIV issued a decree prohibiting Gypsies:

> We call upon our Bailiffs and Seneschals . . . to arrest and cause to be arrested all those who are called Bohemians or Egyptians, their women and children and others of their following; to secure the men to the convicts' chain, to be led to our galleys and to serve there in perpetuity. And in regard to the women and girls, we order them to be shaven on the first occasion that they are found leading the life of Gypsies and that the children unfit to serve on our galleys be taken to the nearest poor-house to be fed and brought up like the other children who are shut up there. And lest the said women continue to roam about and live like Bohemians, to have them flogged and banished out of the Kingdom, all this without any other form of trial [quoted in Clébert, 1961:89–90, italics omitted].

Similarly, for a period of the twentieth century, Jews were prohibited in parts of Europe.

* * *

The seriousness of deviant behavior depends upon the conventionality of both the offender and the victim. The most serious is the deviant behavior of an unconventional person or group against someone more conventional, followed by deviant behavior between people equally conventional, then between people equally unconventional, and lastly by the deviant behavior of a conventional person or group against someone less conventional. All else constant, the quantity of law decreases in this order.

CULTURAL DISTANCE

One kind of cultural distance is a difference in the quantity of culture (as on page 65), and another is a difference in the frequency of culture, or its conventionality (as on page 70). Now consider still another kind, a difference in the content of culture, or cultural diversity. It is possible to measure cultural distance of this kind across every aspect of culture in every social setting. Every difference is a distance, so that people may have religious distance between them, or ideological, moral, linguistic, or aesthetic distance of one kind or another, and all of these together also define cultural distance (see Glenn and Alston, 1968). And just as it is possible to measure stratification or intimacy among a number of people (see pages 13, 41), so the cultural diversity of a larger setting is defined by the cultural distance, on the average, between each person or group and every other, and by the range between those who are farthest apart. It is therefore possible to measure the cultural distance between two people or among a multitude, across societies, communities, neighborhoods, organizations, marriages, friendships, or face-to-face encounters. Moreover, whatever the setting may be, cultural distance of this kind predicts and explains the quantity of law:

> *The relationship between law and cultural distance is curvilinear.*

In other words, law is less likely at the extremes, where there is little or no cultural diversity, and also where it is great. This applies to every expression of law, from its evolution across history, to litigation and adjudication across disputes, to the severity of punishment across cases.

First consider the evolution of law. A society of the simplest kind, such as a band of nomads, has little cultural diversity, and little or no law. It is without subcultures, without cultural conflict, with little creativity or even individuality of the kind seen in a more modern society. Its people have little or no contact with the cultural life of other tribes or societies, apart from people much like themselves. If there is contact with foreigners, however, the cultural distance is likely to be extremely great. Hence, a simple tribe seldom experiences cultural diversity, but when it does, it is enormous.

Across history, the appearance of cultural diversity between these extremes explains the emergence of the state and law (see Fortes and Evans-Pritchard, 1940:9). In Africa, for example, a state emerged among the Ngwato of what is now Botswana, the Zulu of South Africa, the Bemba of Zambia, the Banyankole of Uganda, and the Kede of Nigeria, among others—and every one of these was "an amalgam of different peoples, each aware of its unique origin and history [Fortes and Evans-Pritchard, 1940:9]." By contrast, this did not happen among people such as the Logoli of Kenya, the Tallensi of Ghana, or the Nuer of the Sudan—and each of these was comparatively homogeneous (Fortes and Evans-Pritchard, 1940:9–10). Hold constant all but the diversity of culture, compare societies of every kind, and law is greater where culture is more diverse in the daily life of the people.

As a society modernizes, its culture diversifies. This happened over the centuries in Europe, but in Africa, South America, Oceania, and other places still partly tribal, it happens in a matter of decades at most. Some tribes in these areas had long known one another— through trade or conquest—but from day to day the typical society was a world of its own. Even after the Europeans came it was possible to stay among one's own kind most of the time. Life in the remote village was much as before and, as before, law was rarely seen. The more contact the natives had with Europeans, however, the more law they had. With the arrival of Europeans in Bechuana-land (now Botswana), for example, the Tswana had an explosion of legislation:

> Practically all of the known legislation amongst the Tswana occurred after the initial impact of Western civilization. Assuming that the very scanty information about earlier legislation is not due simply to the absence of records, whether written or traditional, but actually reflects the paucity of such legislation, we may conclude that contact with Europeans created situations that called for the more frequent exercise of the chief's legislative powers . . . . Almost all these laws have been in the spheres of tribal life that were immediately affected by . . . European influences [Schapera, 1943:66].

The diversification of culture was most dramatic in the economic life of the colonies—in the mines, on the plantations, and in the towns and seaports:

> In Burma, as in Java, probably the first thing that strikes the visitor is the medley of peoples—European, Chinese, Indian and native. It is in the strictest sense a medley, for they mix but do not combine. Each group holds by its

own religion, its own culture and language, its own ideas and ways. As individuals they meet, but only in the market-place, in buying and selling. There is a plural society, with different sections of the community living side by side, but separately, within the same political unit . . . . One finds similar conditions all over the Tropical Far East—under Spanish, Portuguese, Dutch, British, French or American rule; among Filipinos, Javanese, Malays, Burmans and Annamese; whether the objective of the colonial power has been tribute, trade or material resources; under direct rule and under indirect. The obvious and outstanding result of contact between East and West has been the evolution of a plural society; in the Federated Malay States the indigenous inhabitants number barely a quarter of the total population. The same thing has happened in the South Pacific . . . . In African dependencies there are Indian immigrants in East Africa and Syrians in West Africa . . . . The plural society has a great variety of forms, but in some form or other it is the distinctive character of modern tropical economy [Furnivall, 1948:304, 305].

And as plural societies of this kind came into being across the world, law increased (see, e.g., Furnivall, 1948:136–137; Epstein, 1953).

The experience of North American tribes was different, but the result was much the same. Not left on their native lands nor recruited to work for Europeans, the Indians were herded onto reservations, with different tribes sometimes finding themselves together for the first time. The Six Nations of the Iroquois were thrown together, for instance: "A Mohawk was likely to be living next to a Cayuga and a Cayuga next to a Tuscarora, and the likelihood of a dispute extending beyond the tribe was greatly increased [Noon, 1949:42]." Out of these conditions arose Iroquois law, applicable to all of the tribes (see Noon, 1949:42). Other Indians took up life among the whites, and the more they intermingled, the more law they experienced.

In a modern society such as the United States, a few enclaves of homogeneity remain, subcultures where law rarely enters, but these are disappearing. It becomes ever harder to live in a cultural capsule, uncontaminated by other ways of life. Cultural differences are everywhere, in the buildings and parks, passing on the streets, in the midst of everything. The old ethnic neighborhoods, last stands of uniformity, fall apart. As this happens, law increases.

The resolution of disputes obeys the same principle as the evolution of law. In medieval England, for instance, law applied to disputes between Jews and gentiles but not to disputes between Jews alone (Pollock and Maitland, 1898: Volume 1, 468–475). In early

nineteenth-century America, law applied to disputes between Indians and whites but not to disputes between Indians alone
(Prucha, 1962:211–212). Today, in an American Chinatown, disputes
between Chinese and non-Chinese are more likely to result in litigation than disputes between fellow Chinese (Grace, 1970). In an Italian neighborhood, the same applies to fellow Italians:

> It is almost impossible to persuade one of them to make a complaint to the
> police; indeed, they shun all public sources of social control. They handle
> grievances, contracts, and exchanges in a very informal manner, usually
> limited to the immediate parties [Suttles, 1968:101–102].

In fact, the same applies, to one degree or another, to fellow ethnics
of all kinds. Just as a person is less likely to bring a lawsuit against a
member of his own ethnic group, he is less likely to call the police,
the police are less likely to make an arrest, and the judge less likely to
convict or to order a severe penalty. A plaintiff against a fellow ethnic
is less likely to win, and if he loses, he is less likely to appeal (see
Epstein, 1958:222–223). If an ethnic injures a member of his own
subculture, the damages he pays are less. Whatever he does, it is less
serious if his victim is like himself. The same principle applies
everywhere, even in a marriage or friendship. A husband and wife
of the same religion are less likely to take their marital dispute to
court, for instance, and a judge is less likely to grant a divorce if they
do.

This principle applies to matters between officials and citizens
as well. Thus, in an American city, an Italian official is more likely to
be lenient with an Italian, a Puerto Rican with a Puerto Rican, a Jew
with a Jew. Scramble these, and law increases, whether by arrest, a
judicial finding, or a parole decision. In an Italian neighborhood, for
instance, an Italian policeman is less likely to arrest an Italian boy
than a black boy, though he may punish the Italian in other ways:

> Often a policeman simply gives a boy "hell" or "takes him in the alley."
> When carried out by a member of one's own ethnic group, this may be
> accepted practice. Otherwise it becomes a cause for great concern and many
> recriminations. The Italian policemen in the Addams area were very cautious
> about handling Negro boys in such an informal way. It was much easier and
> safer just to arrest them [Suttles, 1968:204, note 10].

But recall that the relationship between law and cultural distance is curvilinear. Hence, law also decreases when the distance between an official and a citizen is extremely great, when one is foreign to the other. A policeman or other official is comparatively lenient toward a visitor from another society, for example, a tourist or a diplomat.

Across the world, law has increased as homogeneous cultures have diversified, and as diverse cultures have homogenized. Many settings still very homogeneous, however, such as families, friendships, and tribes, still have little law. And some, still very diverse, have little as well. Great cultural distances still separate many people of African and Oceanian countries, for example, and law rarely appears between them. But these differences are narrowing. People once alien increasingly share a larger world and a larger culture. Differences are everywhere, increasingly, and yet everyone increasingly has something in common. Likewise, although the cultural distances between many nations of the world still remain great, the culture of the world is homogenizing, and international law is increasing (see Barton, 1949:4).

*   *   *

Cultural distance also predicts and explains the style of law— whether it is penal, compensatory, therapeutic, or conciliatory. All else constant, penal law varies directly with cultural distance, whereas conciliatory law varies inversely with cultural distance. For instance, in a matter between people who are members of the same ethnic group, a policeman is more likely to arrange for restitution or a reconciliation between the parties. If the case goes to court, the judge is less likely to punish the offender; he might, for example, allow psychiatric care instead. This applies as well to the style of tribunals and even to the style of law in societies. For instance, case by case, tribal tribunals are less likely than modern tribunals to punish people, and, overall, tribal societies have less penal law than modern societies (compare Durkheim, 1893: Book 1, Chapters 2–6). But where the cultural conditions for penal law are the poorest, they are best for conciliatory law. The best conditions for compensatory and therapeutic law, however, lie between these extremes. Just as the quantity of law varies with the diversity of culture, then, so does its style.

SUBCULTURES AND DEVIANT BEHAVIOR

One theory of deviant behavior explains the motivation of the deviant with his participation in a subculture. Specifically, deviant behavior is seen as conformity to the values of a subculture, so that what is wrong from the standpoint of the larger society is acceptable or even virtuous from the standpoint of the deviant's associates. Subcultural theory has several versions: According to the theory of "differential association," for example, criminality is a result of the favorable definition of crime among the criminal's associates (Sutherland and Cressey, 1960:77–80; see also Sutherland, 1929:107–109). Another theory explains juvenile delinquency as conformity to the values and expectations of the lower-class subculture, a setting that glorifies toughness, excitement, and trouble (Miller, 1958). Yet another explains drug addiction as a result of participation in a subculture where getting high is a virtue (Feldman, 1968). Many folk theories explain deviant behavior in the same way. In American popular thought, for instance, criminality may be explained with the culture of blacks, Puerto Ricans, bohemians, or motorcyclists. The same applies to southern Europeans in northern Europe, Arabs in France, West Indians in England, and Gypsies everywhere.

The facts support these theories, since members of subcultures are overrepresented among those arrested, convicted, and sentenced to prison (see, e.g., Sutherland and Cressey, 1960: Chapters 8–9). The same facts support the theory of law, however: Law varies inversely with the conventionality of the offender (see page 70). This means that, all else constant, members of subcultures are more vulnerable to law of every kind. They are treated more severely when they engage in crime or other illegality, and their conduct is more likely to be defined as illegal in the first place, whether by legislation or—case by case—by complainants and officials such as police and judges. Hence, the theory of law predicts and explains the same facts as the subcultural theory of deviant behavior.

THE BEHAVIOR OF SOCIAL CONTROL

Social control in general varies with the quantity and diversity of culture, and with its location and direction in cultural space. Consider, for example, social control in science.

Social control among scientists is informal and decentralized, rarely involving litigation or formal action of any other kind (see Polanyi, 1946:33–51; Jouvenel, 1961). Hence, rarely does a scientist experience public disgrace, as by censure or dismissal. A scientist is subject primarily to the opinion of his colleagues, and his reputation depends upon what they say about his work:

> Sovereignty over the world of science is vested in no particular ruler or governing body, but is divided into numerous fragments, each of which is wielded by one single scientist. Every time a scientist makes a decision in which he ultimately relies on his own conscience or personal beliefs, he shapes the substance of science or the order of scientific life as one of its sovereign rulers. The powers thus exercised may sharply affect the interests of his fellow scientists [Polanyi, 1946:49].

A scientist's colleagues monitor every aspect of his work, its substance as well as the spirit in which he relates to it. They expect him to be, for instance, objective and disinterested, and they expect him to share his knowledge and discoveries with others (see Merton, 1942:270–278). They expect him to be careful in his work. They call upon him to be original but demand humility if he succeeds (see Merton, 1957). Social control among scientists usually is indirect, often it is subtle, but it is inescapable. The quantity of social control nevertheless varies from one scientific setting to another, so that some scientists are subject to more than others.

Scientific ideas vary quantitatively, and social control among scientists varies directly with them. Thus, as the body of science has grown over time, so has its social control. Over the centuries scientific standards have proliferated and tightened, and the seriousness of scientific misconduct has increased. For example, plagiarism today is more serious than ever before—its consequences are greater. The same applies to false charges of plagiarism, misrepresentation of findings, shoddy workmanship, and other kinds of scientific misconduct. And surveillance among scientists is greater than ever before. It arises in every aspect of scientific life, in universities, research centers, professional associations, informal networks, team projects, and among collaborators and colleagues. Editors and referees of scientific journals also uphold scientific standards, as do awards committees and recruitment and promotion committees. These agencies have grown with the body of science itself; many, in fact, did not even exist in earlier times. Across societies, therefore, those with the most advanced science have the most advanced social control among scientists. And the more developed sciences—such as physics and chemistry—have more social control than primitive sciences—such as sociology, anthropology, and political science. In each field, social control is also greater among the more advanced scientists, as measured by the quantity and success of their ideas, such as their publications and citations in the literature. Elite scientists in major universities and research centers continually scrutinize the quality of their colleagues' work, for instance, whereas those at a lower level, such as unpublished teachers of science, are not so concerned with matters of this kind.

Social control in science also varies with its direction in scientific space: It is greater in a direction toward less scientific status than toward more. Accordingly, a complaint by an advanced scientist against a lesser scientist is both more likely and more serious than a complaint in the opposite direction. In a university or other research setting, for example, deviant behavior by a scientist with many successful publications against a comparatively unpublished scientist is less serious than the reverse. Even if the lesser scientist finds an audience for his complaint, it is less likely that his more prominent colleague will suffer social control. With relatively little risk, therefore, a senior scientist can victimize his junior in one way or another. For example, he can expropriate research findings or other ideas, present them in lectures as his own, or publish them. This may even enhance his reputation all the more. An eminent scientist enjoys a certain immunity, therefore, and the more eminent he is, the more immunity he enjoys (see Merton, 1968). But those without such credentials must be careful of an eminent colleague, since his evaluation counts so much and he can seriously damage their reputations, if not ruin them. All else constant, then, social control in science varies inversely with the prominence of the offender, but it varies directly with the prominence of the complainant. Thus, a student scientist is the most vulnerable, and his complaints mean almost nothing.

Social control among scientists also varies with their conventionality. For instance, among themselves, scientists with conventional ideas have more social control than those with strange or otherwise infrequent ideas. But here the direction of social control is important as well: The conventional scientist holds his unconventional colleague to higher standards than he would apply to those with more popular ideas like his own. And so does everyone else. The misconduct of an unconventional scientist is more serious: His originality is more questionable, his emotionality more inappropriate, his immodesty more obnoxious, his errors more outrageous. The same principle explains why, all else constant, a new idea is more likely to encounter social control than an old idea (compare Barber, 1961). Consequently, in his early days, a scientific pioneer is more likely than others to encounter resistance of all kinds, even ridicule. In this sense, genius can jeopardize a scientist's reputation. If an unconventional scientist should complain about his more conventional colleague, however, this is not so serious. Indeed, the conventional scientist is comparatively immune to him. It is not so serious if the conventional scientist fails to cite the work or otherwise acknowledge the priority of his unconventional colleague. Yet if a scientist with low status of this kind defends himself, as by secretiveness about his ideas or a demand for recognition, his more conventional colleagues define him as all the worse.

Finally, cultural distance also predicts and explains social control among scientists. Among the mass of scientific ideas, some are closer to others in content and style. Distances of this kind define distances between scientists, and these predict and explain social control among them. At the extremes, where their ideas are very similar or very different, social control is weak or absent. It is weak among scientists who do the very same kind of work, for instance, but also among those in different fields altogether. On the other hand, more social control appears among those whose ideas are neither close nor distant but somewhere between, familiar but not second nature, different but not foreign. More appears within scientific specialties than between collaborators, and more within university departments than across them. A scientist's colleagues decide his reputation, then, but generally their knowledge of his work is limited to some degree. Hence, if he is defined as a failure, a scientist may feel that the wrong standards were applied, or that he was not understood.

5

ORGANIZATION

Organization is the corporate aspect of social life, the capacity for collective action (see Weber, 1922b:145–147; Swanson, 1971:621–622; Smith, 1972:254). This is found in any group, whether a couple or a gang of playmates, a club, family, or firm, a political party, municipality, or state. But some groups are more organized than others: Organization is a quantitative variable. Measures of organization include the presence and number of administrative officers, the centralization and continuity of decision making, and the quantity of collective action itself.

The quantity of organization explains many aspects of social life. For instance, an early formulation holds that democracy varies inversely with organization:

> It is organization which gives birth to the dominion of the elected over the electors, of the mandataries over the mandators, of the delegates over the delegators. Who says organization, says oligarchy [Michels, 1911:365].

Organization also explains patterns of revolt. Revolution varies directly with the centralization of the state, for example (see Tocqueville, 1856:204; Moore, 1966:459; Smith, 1966:121), and the same applies to the coup d'état (see Luttwak, 1969: Chapter 2). On the other hand, secession varies inversely with the centralization of the state. Organization also explains religious life, such as the location of gods and other spirits (Fustel de Coulanges, 1864:122–126), their number and functions (Swanson, 1960: Chapters 3–4), and their degree of involvement in everyday life (Swanson, 1967). It explains the success of social movements (see Oberschall, 1973: Chapter 4), science (Ben-David, 1971), and art (Becker, 1974).

Organization explains aspects of law as well. The quantity of law varies with the organization of its environment, its direction in relation to differences in organization, and with the organization of law itself.

THE QUANTITY OF ORGANIZATION

Organization varies in time and space. A society may be more or less organized as a state, for instance, and its people may be more or less organized into smaller groups, whether hunting parties, secret fraternities, clans, voluntary associations, or corporations. One church may be more organized than another, one army more than another, one legal system more than another. Even one individual may be more organized than another—as measured by his memberships. Finally, any group is, by definition, more organized than an individual on his own.

However and wherever it is measured, the capacity for collective action predicts and explains the quantity of law:

Law varies directly with organization.

The organization of a society may increase slowly, over centuries, or over shorter periods of time. It tends to increase during a war, for example, but this may end with the war itself. During a war, the state tends to centralize, and this is true of democratic as well as autocratic regimes:

War does not always give democratic societies over to military government, but it must invariably and immeasurably increase the powers of civil government; it must automatically concentrate the direction of all men and the control of all things in the hands of government . . . . All those who seek to destroy the freedom of the democratic nations must know that war is the surest and shortest means to accomplish this. That is the very first axiom of their science [Tocqueville, 1840:650].

Similarly:

The well-known reciprocal relation between a despotic orientation and the warlike tendencies of a group rests on this formal basis: war needs a centralistic intensification of the group form, and this is guaranteed best by despotism [Simmel, 1908a:88; see also Coser, 1956: Chapter 5].

And during a war law increases. In ancient Rome, for instance, law expanded with the Empire, at home as well as abroad, invading even *patria potestas*, the traditional sovereignty of the Roman father (Nisbet, 1964). War brings legislation and codification (Weber, 1925:84–85, 272). Thus, with the conquest of the Roman Empire came the *leges barbarorum*, or barbarian laws. Likewise, in establishing the Mongolian Empire, Genghis Khan compiled a code, and, six centuries later, so did Napoleon (see Weber, 1925:272). War also brings new legal agencies, emergency powers for old agencies, more surveillance, litigation, and severity.

War brings organization to stateless societies as well, even a kind of state on a temporary basis:

The political unit of tribal society is typically variable in extent. The level of political consolidation contracts and expands: primary segments that unite to attack or repel an enemy at one time may fragment into feuding factions at another, quarreling over land or over personal injuries. Moreover, the degree to which political consolidation proceeds typically depends on circumstances external to the tribe itself. The existence of a well-organized predatory neighbor, or, conversely, the opportunity to prey upon a nearby society, will give impetus to confederation. Local autonomy breaks down, on a greater or lesser scale, proportionate to the amount of—and during the extent of—concerted action possible against other societies. In an uncontested environment, on the other hand, the primary segments of a tribe will show little inclination toward consolidation [Sahlins, 1961:326, italics omitted].

And as this capacity for collective action comes and goes, so does law. Among the Plains Indians of North America, for example, military organization was temporary, and so was law: With war a chief emerged, but with peace his authority faded away (see Lowie, 1948). This was also true of the Jibaros of Equador and Peru:

> The authority of the chief elected for a war is very great. It is he alone who disposes everything for the expedition planned, who decides about the time for and the mode of making the attack, and the younger warriors oblige themselves to obey him in everything. But as soon as a war has been carried to a successful end the power of the chief ceases, and he has, in spite of the great repute he always enjoys, no more authority or right to decide over the doings of his tribesmen than any other family father among the Jibaros [Karsten, 1923:8].

Similar patterns have appeared among stateless people throughout the world. Law varies directly with war, since war implies organization.

Organization also increases with foreign contacts of other kinds, and so do episodes of law. Thus, in North America, the first tribal council of the Comanches was called in order to discuss a treaty with the United States. Until then, no central authority had ever spoken for the numerous Comanche bands (Hoebel, 1940:11). Many Indians who were anarchic among themselves acted through war chiefs or other spokesmen in their dealings with white men, and so the whites came to believe, incorrectly, that all Indians were governed in this way. Law also increases with foreign trade. With the slave trade in Africa, for instance, many people experienced law for the first time (see Weber, 1925:265). On the other hand, many stateless people—such as the Pygmies of Zaire, the Negritos of the Philippines, and the Aborigines of Australia—are isolated deep in the wilderness, beyond the reach of foreigners, and this explains their statelessness: Law varies directly with intersocietal interaction. Like a simple society, the international community is isolated from other worlds, and its law is correspondingly primitive. The many nations have never acted as a single group. Contact with another world, however, surely would awaken international organization, and international law would grow as never before (see Barton, 1949:1–4).

Law increases with collective action within a society as well. For instance, across history, the organization of many societies has increased with irrigation and flood control (Wittfogel, 1957). The building and maintenance of water works involves a centralization of decision making:

> A large quantity of water can be channeled and kept within bounds only by the use of mass labor; and this mass labor must be coordinated, disciplined, and led. Thus a number of farmers eager to conquer arid lowlands and plains are forced to invoke organizational devices which—on the basis of pre-machine technology—offer the one chance of success: they must work in cooperation with their fellows and subordinate themselves to a directing authority . . . .

> No matter whether traditionally nonhydraulic leaders initiated or seized the incipient hydraulic apparatus, or whether the masters of this apparatus became the motive force behind all important public functions, there can be no doubt that in all these cases the resulting regime was decisively shaped by the leadership and social control required by hydraulic agriculture [Wittfogel, 1957:18, 27, quotation marks omitted].

Accordingly, law increases with irrigation. This was true, for instance, in early Egypt, Hawaii, Mesopotamia, China, Peru, and Mexico (Wittfogel, 1957: Chapters 3–7; Sanders, 1968). Law also increases with other public works, at least until the work is done. In the squatter settlements, or *barrios*, of modern Caracas, for instance, law expands during public works such as roadbuilding:

> The dispute-resolving functions of the junta vary from barrio to barrio in positive correlation to the junta's strength and level of activity in promoting community cooperation. A junta that is not organizing roadbuilding or other public-works activities is not likely to try to resolve individual disputes, nor would such a junta's decisions be respected [Karst, Schwartz, and Schwartz, 1973:53].

Similarly, the Indians of North America had police during their occasional public works, such as construction of the great burial mounds of the Ohio Valley (MacLeod, 1937:189). They had police for other kinds of communal action as well, such as the buffalo hunt of the Plains Indians:

> In order to ensure a maximum kill, a police force—either coinciding with a military club, or appointed ad hoc, or serving by virtue of clan affiliation—issued orders and restrained the disobedient. In most of the tribes they not only confiscated game clandestinely procured, but whipped the offender, destroyed his property, and, in case of resistance, killed him. The very same

organization which in a murder case would merely use moral suasion turned into an inexorable State agency during a buffalo drive [Lowie, 1948:18; see also MacLeod, 1937; Llewellyn and Hoebel, 1941:111–113].

The Paiutes of Utah and Nevada had law during the rabbit hunt—a headman whose authority was limited to that occasion (Lowie, 1927:5). Among the Northwest Coast Indians, law increased during the salmon runs (see Service, 1971:137). Northern Eskimos display the same pattern in the winter when they hunt sea mammals such as whales and walruses (Hippler and Conn, 1973:23–26); their law is seasonal (see Mauss, 1905–1906, summarized in Pospisil, 1971:101).

Law follows the rhythm of organization, whatever it is. It may follow the cycle of planting and harvesting, for instance, as among the Apinayé Indians of northern Brazil, who had policemen only during the growing season. Uniformed in special girdles and neckbands, they regulated the planting, care, and harvesting of the crops, known as their "children." One of their duties, for example, was to announce the maturity of the "children." Anyone harvesting before that time was subject to punishment (Nimuendajú, 1939:89–90). In the northern woodlands of America, Indian police punished anyone who prematurely harvested the wild rice (for references, see Lowie, 1948:18). And the early Ontong Javanese had officials, the *polepole*, who guarded against the theft of coconuts and other foodstuffs from the common lands (Hogbin, 1934:210–211).

Yet another occasion for organization is a disaster, such as an earthquake, famine, or epidemic. The Black Death of Europe was such an occasion, for instance, and it was accompanied by a considerable increase of law. "Sanitary councils" appeared throughout Europe, and "plague regulations" of all kinds multiplied. An early statute from fourteenth-century Italy illustrates the pattern:

Everyone sick of the plague is to be brought out of the town to the fields, there to die or recover. Those who have nursed plague patients are to remain secluded for ten days before having intercourse with anyone. The clergy are to examine the sick and report to the authorities on pain of being burnt at the stake and confiscation of their possessions. Those who introduce the plague shall forfeit all their goods to the State. Finally, with the exception of those set apart for the purpose, no one shall administer to those sick of the plague on pain of death and forfeiture of their possessions [quoted in Nohl, 1926:72].

Plague law eventually broadened to prohibit whatever might anger God, such as gambling, drinking, prostitution, and begging (Nohl, 1926:74–75). In early America, law increased during many lesser epidemics (see Bacon, 1939:194). As with war, public works, the hunt, the harvest, or disaster, so with a religious festival (see Mac-Leod, 1937; Lowie, 1948:18). So with a migration (see, e.g., Barth, 1961:76). In the Roman Republic, police—*aediles* and *triumviri capitales*—appeared at the market, the games, and executions, but generally had no other authority (Lintott, 1968:92–106). And law varies directly with planned change of all kinds. In Africa, Latin America, Oceania, and Asia, law increases with the destruction of tradition and the engineering of modern life. It increases with revolutionary change (e.g., Massell, 1968; Berman, 1969). It increases with totalitarianism, the ultimate in planning. Likewise, as planning increases among and across nations, international law increases.

Law varies directly with private as well as public organization, and with informal as well as formal organization. It varies with the number of groups and with the internal structure of groups. The more organizations per capita, for example, the more law. At one extreme is a simple society such as a tribe of hunters or herdsmen, with little organizational life at all, public or private. Compared to a modern society, people of this kind are groupless. They have no economic organizations such as factories or stores, no interest groups or other voluntary associations, no service establishments such as hospitals or schools. They have kinship and peer groups, and possibly age, sex, and residential groups, but little else. People of this kind have little or no law either (see Smith, 1965:42–48; 1966; 1972).

Among themselves, organizations and groups are more litigious than individuals, and the more organized they are, the more litigious they are. Corporations are more litigious than voluntary associations, and the more organized corporations are more litigious than others. It also follows that the litigiousness of individuals varies directly with their memberships and with the organization of the groups to which they belong.

Every aspect of law varies directly with the organization of the parties. An organization bringing a lawsuit against another is more likely to win than an individual bringing a lawsuit against another individual. Between organizations, the loser loses more, an appeal by the plaintiff is more likely, and so is a reversal in its behalf. In fact, many organizations in modern society have so much legal life that they hire lawyers on a permanent basis. But then the law of organizations, especially corporation law, is voluminous. In proportion to their number in the population, organizations have more than their share of law (compare Ladinsky, 1963:54).

ORGANIZATIONAL DIRECTION

Just as rank may be understood as vertical status (see page 16), or integration as radial status (see page 48), so the capacity for collective action may be understood as a kind of status as well. The organizational status of a group is defined by the degree of its organization, that of an individual by his memberships. Moreover, just as law may have vertical direction in relation to differences in rank (see page 21), so it may have organizational direction in relation to differences in organizational status. It may proceed from more to less organization, or from less to more. Its direction is opposite that of the deviant behavior. When a group offends an individual on his own, for example, the direction of law is from less to more organization. In the case of a complaint by a group against an individual, the direction of law is from more to less organization. This predicts and explains differences in the quantity of law:

> Law is greater in a direction toward less
> organization than toward more organization.

All else constant, then, a business or other organization is more likely to complain to the police about an individual than vice versa, and, when this happens, an arrest is more likely, as is a confession, prosecution, conviction, and severe sentence (see Hall, 1952:319). Similarly, a group is more likely to bring a lawsuit against an individual than vice versa, and it is more likely to win (see Galanter, 1975:348–360). In modern America, for instance, the absolute quantity of law is greater in a direction from more to less organization than from less to more: One-half of the plaintiffs in civil litigation are organizations, but two-thirds of the defendants are individuals (Wanner, 1974:423–437). Moreover, "organizations are uniformly more successful than individuals [Wanner, 1975:300]." In small-claims cases as well, more organizations sue individuals than vice versa (see Yngvesson and Hennessey, 1975:235–243). And the plaintiff nearly always wins (see Yngvesson and Hennessey, 1975:243–254). It might also be added that if an organization loses its case against an individual, it is more likely to appeal, and, if it does, it is more likely to win a reversal.

Just as a difference in rank may be understood as vertical distance (see page 24), so a difference in organization may be understood as organizational distance. This also predicts and explains the quantity of law:

> *In a direction toward less organization, law*
> *varies directly with organizational distance.*

But:

> *In a direction toward more organization, law*
> *varies inversely with organizational distance.*

Although any group is more likely to bring a lawsuit against an individual than vice versa, then, the likelihood of a lawsuit by a group increases with its organization. On the other hand, the likelihood of a lawsuit by an individual against a group decreases with the organization of the group. The same principles apply to other measures of law as well, whether the success of a lawsuit, the severity of a punishment, or whatever. It follows that, all else constant—including the victim's organization—law varies inversely with the organization of the offender. And, all else constant—including the offender's organization—law varies directly with the organization of the victim. First consider the offender.

Organization provides an immunity from law, and the more organized the offender, the more of this immunity is enjoyed. In other words, an offense committed by an organization or its representative is less serious than an offense by an individual on his own, and the more organized the organization, the less serious it is. In a modern society such as the United States, for example, much criminal conduct by organizations lies within the jurisdiction of such regulatory agencies as the Federal Trade Commission, the Securities and Exchange Commission, and the Environmental Protection Agency (for an overview, see Davis, 1969). These agencies are more lenient than agencies dealing with criminal conduct by individuals. A regulatory agency is more likely to give an organization another chance, such as by allowing it to avoid punishment in return for a promise to conform in the future. An organization's word is better than an individual's.

During World War II, for example, the United States Office of Price Administration issued and enforced a vast number of price, rent, and distribution regulations. Many criminal violations by businesses were recognized, but few were punished, and, of those, few were punished severely:

> The length of some of the sentences imposed on businessmen who had willfully violated the OPA regulations—and in so doing made large sums of money—were almost trivial compared with the sentences given offenders who violated ordinary criminal laws pertaining to property offenses . . . . During 1944, there were actions in 322,131 cases of violation. Warnings or other informal adjustments, including dismissals, were issued in 271,874 cases, or 84 per cent of the total cases. In the remaining 16 per cent of the cases, administrative action was used in 26,763, and court proceedings were instituted in 28,903 cases . . . . Criminal prosecution was begun by the Department of Justice against 3,934 defendants [a little more than 1 percent of all cases] [Clinard, 1946:263–265, punctuation edited].

It might be added that the typical case handled by a regulatory agency originates with a citizen's complaint, the likelihood of which also decreases as the organization of the offender increases. Thus, a citizen is less likely to complain about a fraudulent act by an individual representing an organization than to complain about the same offense by an individual on his own, and the more organized the organization represented, the less likely is a complaint of this kind. Assuming that the organization of a group increases with its size, for instance (see Blau, 1970:213–216), the likelihood of a complaint varies inversely with the size of an organization (see, e.g., Steele, 1975:1127). If a complaint is brought against it, moreover, a larger organization is less likely to lose the case. Over a number of years in the United States, for example, a large union of garment workers won over three-fourths of its arbitration cases against a small association of dress manufacturers, but another large union won only a little over one-third of its cases against a large automobile manufacturer (Evan, 1959:9). The same principle explains why it is so difficult to win a lawsuit against a modern state.

Now consider the victim. The more organized the victim of a crime, for instance, the more serious is the offense. Accordingly, the police are more likely to hear about a robbery of a business than a robbery of an individual on the street. If they do, they are more likely to make an investigation and an arrest, prosecution is more likely, and so is a conviction and a severe sentence. The same applies to all crime. In the United States, for example, theft from a department store by a customer or an employee has a conviction rate of nearly 100 percent of the cases prosecuted (Cameron, 1964:142; Robin, 1967:696). But for auto theft—almost always a crime against an individual—this rate is only a little over 50 percent (U.S. Federal Bureau of Investigation, 1974:28). Also lower are the conviction rates for crimes against individuals such as rape, aggravated assault, and murder (U.S. Federal Bureau of Investigation, 1974:10, 12, 15).

Just as a robbery of a business is more serious than that of an individual, so a robbery of a supermarket is more serious than that of a small grocery store. All the more serious is a crime against the state. Thus, in the United States, embezzlement from the Post Office Department is more serious than embezzlement from a private business (see Hall, 1952:319–330). In the Soviet Union as well, any theft from the state is more serious than other theft:

> The planned economy protects itself . . . by imposing very severe penalties for the theft of socialist property, as contrasted with the theft of personal property of individuals. By a law of August 7, 1932, social (state, collective-farm or co-operative) property was declared to be "sacred and inviolable," and persons making an attempt on it were "to be considered enemies of the people." By this law theft of social property was punishable by death by

shooting unless committed under mitigating circumstances . . . . Theft of
personal property was only punishable by deprivation of liberty for a term of
up to three months, and theft by assault (robbery) by deprivation of liberty
for a term of up to five years [Berman, 1963:148].

This difference eventually narrowed—as Soviet organization relaxed—but it did not disappear. A modern state is more organized than any of its adversaries, and so it has an advantage at every step in the legal process. This is especially striking in criminal cases, as in modern America, where the typical defendant ultimately pleads guilty, giving the state a victory by default (see, e.g., Mileski, 1971:492–496).

Some states are more organized than others, however, and criminal law varies accordingly. Since centralization is a measure of organization, for instance, criminal law varies directly with the centralization of the state. Thus, the likelihood of a complaint to the police increases with the centralization of the criminal process, and the same applies to arrest and conviction. And the more centralized the state, the greater is the severity of punishment (Durkheim, 1899–1900:32–35). The government of ancient Rome became more centralized as it evolved into an empire, for example, and the severity of punishment increased proportionately, with more capital crimes, more burning at the stake, crucifixion, mutilation, and other torture (Durkheim, 1899–1900:40–41). In England as well, the history of capital punishment corresponded to the history of centralization (Baumgartner, 1973:10). Execution was practically unknown under William the Conqueror in the eleventh century, but it grew steadily more frequent and more cruel as authority concentrated in the monarchy, reaching its height under the Tudors and Stuarts in the sixteenth and early seventeenth centuries and declining thereafter (see Baumgartner, 1973:2–10).

As the organization of criminal law increases, the demand for law increases, and it intrudes ever deeper into society, with ever more conduct defined as criminal and ever more violations discovered. Where witchcraft is illegal, for instance, the discovery of witches varies directly with the organization of the witch hunt. Thus, during the Renaissance of Europe, witch hunting was more centralized on the Continent than in England, and proportionately more people on the Continent were charged with the crime of witch-craft, tortured, convicted, and executed (see Currie, 1968:25, 27). People on the Continent were also more likely to confess their witch-craft (see Currie, 1968:13–14, 19). Similarly, in modern societies, an accused person is more likely to cooperate with an autocratic regime than with a democratic or other less centralized regime. And the most cooperative of all is the prisoner of a totalitarian regime:

> The disturbing factor in the success of totalitarianism is . . . the true selfless-ness of its adherents: it may be understandable that a Nazi or Bolshevik will not be shaken in his conviction by [government actions] against people who do not belong to the movement or are even hostile to it; but the amazing fact is that neither is he likely to waver . . . if he becomes a victim of persecution himself, if he is framed and condemned, if he is purged from the party and sent to a forced-labor or a concentration camp. On the contrary, to the wonder of the whole civilized world, he may even be willing to help in his own prosecution and frame his death sentence if only his status as a member of the movement is not touched [Arendt, 1958:307].

* * *

It is possible to rank the seriousness of deviant behavior accord-ing to its organizational location and direction. Among the several possibilities, deviant behavior by an individual against an organiza-tion is the most serious. Next is deviant behavior by one organiza-tion against another, then by an individual against another indi-vidual, and last is deviant behavior by an organization against an individual. In modern America, for instance, a complaint of racial discrimination by a civil-rights group against an individual landlord is the most likely to succeed, a complaint by a civil-rights group against an organization such as a corporation is next most likely, followed by a complaint of an individual on his own against an individual landlord, and finally by a complaint of an individual against an organization (see Mayhew, 1968:235–242, 254–255). Suc-cess in litigation of all kinds follows the same order (see Wanner, 1975:302).

* * *

Organization also predicts and explains the style of law, whether it is penal, compensatory, therapeutic, or conciliatory. For instance, penal law is greater in a direction toward less organization than toward more. This means that an individual's offense against an organization is more likely to be defined as a crime than an organization's offense against an individual. Thus, much so-called "white-collar crime" by corporations is not, in fact, crime (compare Sutherland, 1940). Even when its conduct is subject to the criminal process, punishment of a modern corporation or its representatives is less likely than punishment of an individual for the same offense (see Sutherland, 1945:132–138). White-collar crime is less serious:

> White collar crime is similar to juvenile delinquency in respect to the differential implementation of the law. In both cases, the procedures of the criminal law are modified so that the stigma of crime will not attach to the offenders. The stigma of crime has been less completely eliminated from juvenile delinquents than from white collar criminals because the procedures for the former are a less complete departure from conventional criminal procedures, because most juvenile delinquents come from a class with low social status, and because the juveniles have not organized to protect their good names [Sutherland, 1945:138].

Moreover, in a direction from more to less organization, penal law varies directly with organizational distance. In a direction from less to more organization, penal law varies inversely with organizational distance. All else constant, therefore, penal law varies directly with the organization of the state (see Wilson, 1973:19–20). The more centralized the state, for example, the more its deviants are defined as criminals (see Durkheim, 1899–1900:32–37; Wittfogel, 1957:138–139). The more organized the deviant in relation to the victim, however, the less penal is law. Instead, a deviant group is more likely to be asked to compensate its victim, and the likelihood of this increases with its organization. It is also more likely to be asked to enter into negotiations in order to find a compromise with its victim. Thus, in modern America, rarely do complainants to a consumer fraud bureau demand punishment of a business or its representatives; the great majority want only restitution, performance of a contract, its cancellation, or some other settlement of their loss (Steele, 1975:1138). Therapeutic law, like penal law, is also more likely for an individual on his own. And it varies directly with the organization of the state. In a totalitarian society, for instance, an opponent of the state is more likely to be sent to prison, or to a hospital for treatment.

ORGANIZATION AND DEVIANT BEHAVIOR

Every theory of deviant behavior assumes that deviant behavior is the behavior of individuals (Reiss, 1966:3). Every theory explains deviant behavior with the conditions that motivate an individual to deviate. In one theory the explanation is deprivation (see page 30); in another it is marginality (see page 54); in another, participation in a subculture (see page 79). Since none considers that an organization or other group might engage in deviant behavior, none explains deviant behavior with the conditions of organizational life.

Individuals on their own actually are the subjects of most law enforcement, and so, in this sense, they are more deviant than organizations, especially in regard to crime. Organizations appear in crime statistics as victims of crime but rarely as offenders. Hence, the assumption of deviant behavior theory that individuals, not organizations, are the deviants is justified by the facts. The theory of law, however, predicts and explains the same facts: Law varies inversely with the organization of the offender (see page 93). The official records would show more deviant behavior by organizations if law were to respond to it in the same way as to the conduct of individuals. For instance, over a period of 50 years, 70 of the largest corporations in the United States are known to have engaged in much conduct that might have caused individuals to be stigmatized as criminals:

The tabulation of the crimes of the 70 largest corporations in the United States [excluding public-utility and petroleum companies] gives a total of 980 adverse decisions. Every one of the 70 corporations has a decision against it, and the average number of decisions is 14.0. Of these 70 corporations, 98 per cent are recidivists; that is, they have two or more adverse decisions. Several states have enacted habitual criminal laws, which define an habitual criminal as a person who has been convicted four times of felonies. If we use this number and do not limit the convictions to felonies, 90 per cent of the 70 largest corporations in the United States are habitual criminals. Sixty of the corporations have decisions against them for restraint of trade, 54 for infringements [of patents, copyrights, and trademarks], 44 for unfair labor practices, 27 for misrepresentation in advertising, 26 for rebates, and 43 for miscellaneous offenses [Sutherland, 1948:80].

During World War II, many organizations are known to have violated regulations of the Office of Price Administration, also without the consequences that might have befallen individuals:

> Total violations of OPA regulations by business concerns, both retail and pre-retail [have] undoubtedly been a large figure. Violations of this type uncovered during 1944 alone numbered 338,029. This figure represents violations by approximately 11 per cent of the business firms of the United States . . . . The estimate of about one out of ten business concerns in violation is undoubtedly too low, [since] not all concerns were investigated. Of those investigated, approximately 57 per cent were found in violation [Clinard, 1946:264, punctuation edited; see also page 94 of this volume].

Law is less likely to respond to organizational conduct as deviant, less likely to define it as criminal, and, even if so defining it, less likely to handle it as serious. The theory of law thus predicts and explains the facts that the theory of deviant behavior assumes.

It might be noted that one theory not only assumes that deviant behavior is the behavior of individuals rather than of organizations; it also predicts that an individual is more likely to victimize an organization than to victimize another individual. The explanation is that an individual can more easily "neutralize" the offense in his own mind if his victim is an organization rather than a person (see Sykes and Matza, 1957). He may believe, for instance, that an offense against an organization is less injurious, that it is justified by the organization's own conduct toward individuals, that everybody does it, or that it is not really wrong, or at least not really criminal. Because of such feelings, deviant behavior against an organization is more acceptable to him (see Lofland, 1969:84–93). For the same reasons, a large organization is more acceptable as a victim than a small organization (see Smigel, 1956). In fact, a disproportionate amount of conduct defined as illegal is committed by individuals against organizations. But here again the theory of law predicts and explains the same pattern: An organization is more likely than an individual to make a complaint about an individual, and it is also more likely to complain about an individual than about another organization. Indeed, all else constant, an offense by an individual against an organization is the most serious of the several possible offenses that might involve an organization (see page 97). This means that it is the most likely to result in a call to the police, an arrest, prosecution, conviction, and every other kind of law. For that matter, it is the most likely to be defined as illegal in the first place and, specifically, to be defined as a crime (see page 98).

THE BEHAVIOR OF SOCIAL CONTROL

In general, social control varies directly with organization, and, in general, it is greater in a direction from more to less organization than from less to more. This applies, for instance, to social control within an organization, such as a voluntary association, business, school, army, or prison. For these purposes, a group is an organization if it has one or more administrative officers (see Weber, 1922b:146, 150–151; compare, e.g., Scott, 1964:486–488). Social control in a group of this kind is bureaucracy (see Weber, 1922a:196–198). Moreover, bureaucracy is a quantitative variable: Some organizations have more rules and regulations than others, more complaints, hearings, dismissals, and other penalties. Some have a standard procedure for practically everything; others are loose and flexible.

Bureaucracy varies directly with organization. The more centralized an organization is, for instance, the more rules and regulations it has (see Udy, 1965:699), and the greater is its reaction to deviant behavior. Accordingly, a military unit has more social control than a factory, a factory more than a labor union, a labor union more than a social club. So-called "military law" increases during a war, with more kinds of deviant behavior, more trials, and more severe punishments. Similarly, in the life of a labor union, social control increases during a strike (see Simmel, 1908a:88; compare Olson, 1965:70–72). A more organized religion has more "ecclesiastical law." A more organized political party has more discipline, with a revolutionary party having the most of all (see Selznick, 1952:25–29). With struggle, discipline tightens; dictatorships arise to fight dictatorships, and bureaucracy appears among anarchists.

Bureaucracy is greater in a direction toward less organization than toward more. This means, for instance, that a member has more obligations to his organization than it has to him. He is also less likely to complain about its conduct than vice versa. In a dispute with his organization, he is more likely to lose. If he loses, he is more likely to suffer a severe penalty. But he is more likely to capitulate anyway, to admit that he, not the organization, is wrong. It should also be noted that the more organized the organization, the more obligations a member has to it, the fewer it to him. A member is therefore more accountable to an organization such as an army than to a less centralized organization such as a university.

The style of bureaucracy also varies with organization (compare Etzioni, 1961; 1965). For instance, the penal style is greater in a direction toward less organization than toward more. Punishment thus is more likely when the organization is a victim of its member than vice versa. All else constant, moreover, the penal style of bureaucracy varies directly with the capacity for collective action itself, such as the centralization of the organization (compare Gouldner, 1954:232–233). Just as an army has more bureaucracy than most other organizations, its bureaucracy is more penal: It is more likely than other organizations to punish its deviants, and all the more during a war. Organization explains why some factories are more penal than others, some schools or prisons more than others. Among the most penal are those organizations that embrace their members 24 hours a day, or "total institutions" (Goffman, 1961a:4), such as homes for the aged, concentration camps, ships, and monasteries. All are highly centralized, and all have a penal style of social control. The prison is an extreme example; but each total institution is a prison to some degree, with patterns of discipline usually applied only to children and animals (Goffman, 1961a:50–53). Increase the centralization of decision making in any organization—a mental hospital, university, or holiday resort—and it becomes more like a prison. By contrast, an organization offending its own member is more likely to provide him with compensation of some kind, and nothing more. Or it may negotiate a compromise, without accepting responsibility or blame. On the other hand, therapy is more likely to be prescribed for an individual than for an organization. This is not to deny that an organization may be defined as a victim of circumstance, again with no one to blame for its misconduct. It may even have a pathology and need the help of a consultant (see, e.g., Barnard, 1946).

Organization also explains social control in more informal settings, such as families and peer groups. The social control of children, for instance, increases with the involvement of their parents in organizational life, so that the children of a military man, policeman, or other government employee have more social control than those of an independent professional or farmer, and those of a corporation manager more than those of a small entrepreneur (see Miller and Swanson, 1958: Chapters 2, 4, 8). And children in autocratic or other centralized societies have more social control than those in democratic or other less centralized societies. A centralized family such as a patriarchy has more social control than a more democratic family. But no matter how organized it is from day to day, a family engaged in collective action temporarily increases its social control. Family discipline may therefore assert itself when it is least welcome, such as on the way to a picnic or other outing. A centralized family is also more penal in its style of social control. Hence, as the patriarchal family disappears from the modern world, and children and parents become colleagues, corporal punishment disappears as well (see Miller and Swanson, 1958: Chapters 1, 8).

Social control among children themselves also varies with organization. When they play a game, for example, their demands upon each other increase. Make-believe or hide-and-seek has its own discipline, and football or baseball has all the more. Boys have more collective life than girls, and so they have more social control among themselves, more complaining, ridicule, and other punishment. But this varies from one age to the next, and, accordingly, the moral life of children develops as they grow up (compare Piaget, 1932).

6

SOCIAL CONTROL

Social control is the normative aspect of social life. It defines and responds to deviant behavior, specifying what ought to be: What is right or wrong, what is a violation, obligation, abnormality, or disruption (compare Ross, 1901; Hollingshead, 1941). Law is social control (see pages 2–6), but so are etiquette, custom, ethics, bureaucracy, and the treatment of mental illness. Just as law is social control among the citizens of a state, so the members of a tribe have their own social control, as do the members of a family, workplace, church, clique, or game. Social control is found wherever and whenever people hold each other to standards, explicitly or implicitly, consciously or not: on the street, in prison, at home, at a party. It divides people into those who are respectable and those who are not; it disgraces some, but protects the reputations of others.

Social control is a quantitative variable. One setting has more than another—be it a community, organization, family, friendship, or other relationship. One has more complaints, for instance, more punishments, more severe punishments. One time has more social control than another, be it an epoch or century, a year, season, day, or hour. Moreover, case by case, one kind of social control is greater in magnitude than another. Thus, in modern societies, law is generally greater than other kinds, since it generally responds more to the deviant behavior in its jurisdiction. Legal punishments, for example, are generally defined as more severe than bureaucratic or informal punishments. And one style of social control is greater than another, with penal control generally the greatest, followed by therapeutic, compensatory, and conciliatory control. This also varies across settings of every kind.

Social control explains other aspects of social life. By assuming that people obey the expectations of others, for example, it is possible to explain differences in conduct with differences in social control (see, e.g., Sumner, 1906; Blake and Davis, 1964). Social control explains the conduct of people in organizations (e.g., Etzioni, 1961), neighborhoods (e.g., Suttles, 1968), public places (e.g., Goffman, 1963), and face-to-face encounters (e.g., Goffman, 1956). And one kind of social control explains another, including law. Thus, assuming that legal officials and citizens obey the expectations of others, it is possible to explain differences in law with other social control. For example, it is possible to explain police behavior with departmental expectations (e.g., Skolnick, 1966), the expectations of colleagues (Westley, 1953), neighborhoods (Whyte, 1955:136–139), or communities (Banton, 1964). Social control among citizens may even prohibit law itself. For instance, among the Pedi of South Africa, to bring a lawsuit in the white man's court is "the greatest treason" (Sansom, 1972:193). The Bunyoro of colonial Uganda viewed any lawsuit as "unneighborly" (Beattie, 1957:194). A similar view is held by businessmen in modern America: "One doesn't run to lawyers . . . because one must behave decently [Macaulay, 1963:61]." To call the police, or even to cooperate with them, may also be deviant. It follows that an absence of social control explains deviant behavior. An absence of family or other informal control, for instance, explains juvenile delinquency (e.g., Thrasher, 1927:65; see also pages 9–10). Or, since social control deters deviant behavior, an absence of law explains crime of various kinds (e.g., Andenaes, 1966; Chambliss, 1967). Another kind of theory, however, makes no claim that people obey the expectations of others. Rather, it explains deviant behavior with social control itself: Social control motivates the deviant to deviate all the more (e.g., Lemert, 1967; see also pages 117–118 of this chapter).

Finally, social control also explains deviant behavior and other social life without regard to motivation of any kind (see pages 7–8). Just as it is possible to explain law with the quantity of stratification or organization, for instance (see pages 13–16, 86–92), so it is possible to do this with the quantity of other social control. Respectability, another aspect of social control, explains the behavior of law as well. This includes the quantity of respectability itself, the direction of law between differences in respectability, and the magnitude of these differences. First, consider the quantity of other social control.

THE QUANTITY OF SOCIAL CONTROL

Law is stronger where other social control is weaker (see also pages 6–7):

Law varies inversely with other social control.

This principle explains many known facts, predicts others, and implies a number of earlier formulations.

In rural Mexico, for instance, one community has more family control than another, and this explains why its marital disputes are less likely to go to court:

Patterns of authority seem to be central to an understanding of the distribution of conflict resolution in these towns. In both communities, husbands and wives in conflict recognize the authority of senior family males as well as the authority of the community court. However, in our judgment, the authority of senior family males is greater in the Chiapas town than in the Oaxaca community, and this contrast is mirrored in the use spouses make of the courts in the two towns . . . . In the Oaxaca town, limited authority of senior family males is associated with early inheritance, separate residence, readily available substitutes for both spouses and parents with respect to sex and subsistence, and the deliberate refusal of families to accept responsibility for marriages they have not arranged. The court assumes the responsibility lost or abandoned by the family and exercises authority over marriage vested in it as a representative of the State. In the Chiapas community, delayed inheritance, patrisponsored residence, and the absence of spouse- or parent-

substitutes outside these relationships tend to support the authority of senior
male lineals in the resolution of conflict between spouses. The role that the
court plays is residual [Nader and Metzger, 1963:589, 591].

On the other hand, in nearly all societies the family has more social
control of its own than other groups and relationships, and so, in
general, its disputes are less likely to go to law. In seventeenth-
century America, for example, members of the same family rarely
took one another to court, whereas neighbors more often did (see,
e.g., Demos, 1970a:49). In modern America as well, family disputes
are less likely to go to law than disputes of other kinds, and the
stronger the family, the less likely this is. The police are less likely to
hear about a crime within a family than a crime between strangers
who have no other social control of their own. If the police hear about
a crime within a family, they are less likely to recognize it as such,
whether by writing an official report (Black, 1970:740–741) or by
making an arrest (Black, 1971:1097–1098). It is less likely to be prosecuted (Hall, 1952:318), and, if it goes to court, a conviction is less
likely. Even if convicted, an offender against a member of his own
family is less likely to receive a severe sentence (see also page 42).
But some families have more social control than others, and their
members have all the more immunity from law. Thus, the more
parental control to which a juvenile is subject, the less likely he is to
be subject to law (e.g., Werthman and Piliavin, 1967:73; see also
pages 9–10 of this volume).

In modern societies such as America, however, family control is
weaker than in more traditional societies. With modernization it has
weakened everywhere, and everywhere law has correspondingly
increased. In Taiwan, for instance, the *tsu*, or clan, has steadily lost
its former authority. Its sanctions have been undermined by changes
in land tenure, and the growth of economic relationships outside the
village has made its jurisdiction less relevant anyway. Other social
control in the village has also declined. As all of this has happened,
Taiwanese peasants have more and more turned to the police and
courts (Gallin, 1966). The same pattern has appeared in every part of
the world, gradually in some societies, quickly, even suddenly in
others. In Europe, it happened over centuries. For many Indians of
North America, it happened almost overnight, as quickly as they

were moved to reservations (see, e.g., Noon, 1949:109–110; see also page 76 of this volume). In most of Africa, Asia, Latin America, and Oceania, it has come only recently, if at all. In Africa, for instance, family control is still so strong that juvenile law hardly exists. Thus, in Ethiopia, the first juvenile law was passed only in 1947 (Lowenstein, 1969:49). In Lesotho, Botswana, and Swaziland, juvenile courts still did not exist as late as 1969 (Leslie, 1969:183–184).

Law also varies with every other kind of social control. Thus, it varies across the centuries, growing as every kind of social control dies away—not only in the family but in the village, church, workplace, and neighborhood (Pound, 1942; see also Selznick, 1963; Fuller, 1969). And law varies across societies and across communities and other settings in a single society. In Israel, for example, it varies across the *kibbutzim*, or agricultural settlements. In a *kvutza*, or communal settlement, there is much social control of an informal kind, such as ridicule, scolding, and ostracism, but little or no law. In a *moshav*, however, where families are scattered in separate dwellings, informal control across the settlement is much weaker, and so there is more law (Schwartz, 1954). In any setting where people closely watch each other's conduct and readily criticize and punish deviants in their own way, law is less important. Such a place, for instance, is rural Wales, with kinfolk and neighbors constantly evaluating one another and groups of young men harassing offenders by stuffing their chimneys with straw, dropping dead vermin in their windows, throwing cow dung at them, or other tactics (Rees, 1950:80–84, 126–130; Peters, 1972:109–124). By contrast, among the residents of La Laja, a *barrio* in Ciudad Guayana, Venezuela, social control is almost a matter of law or nothing:

> One way of describing the situation as to informal social controls in La Laja is to say that the social structure is too loosely meshed to cage anyone, that it is generally impossible to mobilize in the community a group large enough or united enough to force any sanction on the deviate. He who is disapproved of is disapproved of by individuals and clusterings of individuals; they may stare and they may talk, but the obstreperous individual will still find others to be his supporters, and he will be barred from no community facilities . . . . A corollary of the weakness of informal controls in the barrio is the fact that when people *do* "involve themselves" in quarrels with their neighbors, they are quite likely to call in the police . . . . The lack of well-organized mechanisms of informal social control makes it natural for the

barrio to resort to the impersonal mechanisms provided by the larger society, even in fairly trivial or rather personal cases [Peattie, 1968:57, 59, 60].

If, for any reason, a citizen is free of other social control, he is more likely to find himself in court or even in prison. In Laos, for example, a Thai typically is subject to less informal control than a Lao, and so he is more vulnerable to law. If a Lao has trouble with another Lao, they go to the *naiban,* or village headman, who acts as a mediator. If the *naiban* is unable to settle the matter it may go to the *tasseng,* an informal leader of several villages. Only if the *tasseng* fails does the case go to a government official, and this is very rare. Under the same conditions, however, a Thai is subject only to law. This explains why, in recent years, the majority of prisoners in the Vientiane jail have been Thai, though the vast majority of citizens in that province were Lao (see Westermeyer, 1971, especially pages 567–568). In modern Africa, residence and tribe may have the same implications: If a case extends beyond the family the parties may resort to village elders, or to another informal tribunal of some kind (e.g., Middleton, 1956; Beattie, 1957; Gulliver, 1963), but an outsider is not subject to these mechanisms, and so he is more vulnerable to law (e.g., Beidelman, 1967:39; see also pages 40–45, 73–78 of this volume). In more modern societies as well, some people are subject to more social control from day to day, and this gives them a degree of immunity from law. Such a person, for example, is a soldier or a sailor; also a priest or monk: Thus, other social control explains the medieval English doctrine known as "benefit of clergy," by which a clergyman who committed an otherwise serious crime was subject only to ecclesiastical authority (see Pollock and Maitland, 1898: Volume 1, 433–457; see also page 66 of this volume).

The quantity of social control varies across settings of all kinds: For example, private settings have more social control than public settings, and less law. An organization with its own security system also has less law. A friendship has less than a more casual relationship (see also pages 40–45). And law even varies with the hours of the clock. When people go to sleep, for instance, most social control relaxes as well, and law increases:

Night is the time for police activities par excellence . . . . The rigidity of public controls during the sleep period is probably related to the break-down of informal controls. When interaction ceases, there are no other sanctions left than official threats or physical manipulation. During the night the legal structure of society is laid bare, stripped of the complex system of informal social controls that are the meat and blood around the skeleton of law in daytime [Aubert and White, 1959:197].

NORMATIVE LOCATION

Just as social control defines who is deviant, it defines who is respectable. Respectability is a quantitative variable, known by the social control to which a group or person has been subject: The more social control, the less respectable he is. Thus, to be subject to law is, in general, more unrespectable than to be subject to other kinds of social control (see pages 105–106). To be subject to criminal law is especially unrespectable, and the more serious the crime, the more unrespectable it is.

In early England, colonial America, and other societies, a criminal might be stigmatized for life: He might be branded with a hot iron, have his nose slit or his ears cut off, or be mutilated in some other way (see, e.g., Pike, 1873:211–213; 1876:280–282, 295; Powers, 1966: Chapter 6; see also Erikson, 1966:196–198). In traditional India, respectability was defined in terms of purity and pollution, with penance the only way an offender could purify himself (see Bühler, 1886: Chapter 11; Orenstein, 1968). So in many societies, a man may "tarnish," "stain," or "taint" his reputation by deviant behavior, but he may also "cleanse" his name in one way or another. A bad reputation, however, may linger forever.

Respectability is normative status. Like rank, or vertical status (see page 16), and integration, or radial status (see page 48), it is a variable in its own right (compare Dahrendorf, 1968a). Someone who is high in rank and well integrated, or with other status, may also be very respectable, but not necessarily so. Anyone can lose his respectability, or damage it. On the other hand, a man may be poor, for instance, or unemployed, but still have respectability. It might be noted that, as with other kinds of status, normative status is partly defined by that of a person's associates, such as members of his family, his friends, or his fellow employees. Hence, a single deviant act may disgrace a whole group, ruining a family name, even for generations, or damaging the reputation of an organization and its members.

Moreover, just as people have different kinds of vertical or radial status, each kind of social control defines its own normative status, each lowering the respectability of any group or person subject to it (compare Garfinkel, 1956). Hence, someone may have a bad reputation from the standpoint of one kind of social control but not another. A man may have a criminal record, for instance, and so have little or no respectability from the standpoint of law, but he may be a good family man, friend, or neighbor. So for a school record, work record, or military record. Or an individual may have a good reputation everywhere but in his own home. Finally, it should be clear that, even though a group or person may have different normative statuses in different settings, these add up to a general reputation in social life. Separately and together, then, many kinds of social control define respectability.

Law varies with its location in normative space, as measured by the respectability of the people in its environment. The more respectable they are, the greater is the quantity of law:

Law varies directly with respectability.

Thus, all else constant, unrespectable people among themselves have less law than more respectable people among themselves. Ex-convicts, for example, are less likely to complain to the police about each other than are more respectable people. So are outcasts of every kind—whoever lives in disrepute. Among themselves, prostitutes are less likely to call the police, as are gamblers, homosexuals, and drug addicts. A professional thief is unlikely to call the police, no matter what happens (Sutherland, 1937:10–12; see also Shaw, 1930:99). In fact, the underworld itself is a normative location, with everyone in it disreputable (see Asbury, 1928:16). So is a prison or mental hospital.

Even if an unrespectable person invokes law against another, he is less likely to succeed. In this sense, a crime by one unrespectable person against another is less serious. The police are less likely to make an investigation or arrest. Prosecution is less likely, as is a conviction or a severe sentence. Robbery of an habitual drunk, for instance, is less serious than the same crime against a more respectable person; so is any crime against a gambler, homosexual, or narcotics addict. A crime against anyone with "dirty hands" is less serious:

> In some situations a crime is committed upon a person who is himself engaged in criminal conduct at the time. . . . Despite the fact that the criminal activity of the victim would not be a defense in a criminal prosecution of the other party, the police are reluctant to arrest in such cases. The most frequently observed situation of this kind is that in which a man has been tricked out of funds given to a prostitute or pimp . . . . Those officers who refuse to take action in these cases probably do so in part because they know that such a case cannot be successfully prosecuted. It is not likely that a warrant will be issued if the complainant does not have "clean hands," and judges are reluctant to convict in cases of this kind [LaFave, 1965:124].

In every way, then, a crime between unrespectable people has fewer risks for the offender. And this applies to all legal matters. An unrespectable person is less likely to bring a lawsuit of any kind against another of his own normative status. If he does, he is less likely to win. Respectable people win more compensation from one another. They are more likely to appeal if they lose a lawsuit and to win a reversal if they do. The more respectable they are, the more law they have. But now consider cases in which one party is more respectable than the other.

NORMATIVE DIRECTION

Like other kinds of status, normative status has its own privileges and disabilities. In modern America, for example, a man who has been convicted of a crime is less likely to find employment, and, though the difference is smaller, so is someone who has been accused but not convicted (Schwartz and Skolnick, 1962; see also Irwin, 1970:135–137). A police record, and every other record of social control, has disabilities as well. Among these are legal disabilities. Just as law varies with its vertical direction (see pages 21–28), or with its radial direction (see pages 49–53), it varies with its normative direction.

A deviant act has normative direction if the offender is less respectable than his victim, or vice versa. The normative direction of law is opposite that of the deviant act. Thus, if a deviant act is from less to more respectability, the normative direction of law is from more to less. This predicts and explains the quantity of law:

Law is greater in a direction toward less
respectability than toward more respectability.

All else constant, then, the less respectable party is more likely to be subject to law, and he is less likely to have its benefits. A complaint by a respectable party against an unrespectable party is more likely than the reverse, and it is more likely to succeed in every way. In a lawsuit, a more respectable party is more likely to win. From a legal standpoint, his case is better. In a criminal case, the word of an unrespectable party means less than that of a legal official or other more respectable party. An arrest, prosecution, or conviction is more likely if the alleged offender is less respectable than the victim, rather than vice versa, and so is a severe sentence. But such a defendant is less likely to appeal and, if he does, less likely to win a reversal.

In medieval England, for instance, a man declared an outlaw was the ultimate in unrespectability. He was vulnerable to everyone, but had no rights of his own:

> He is a "lawless man" and a "friendless man." Of every proprietary, pos-
> sessory, contractual right he is deprived; the king is entitled to lay waste his
> land and it then escheats to his lord; he forfeits his chattels to the king; every
> contract, every bond of homage or fealty in which he is engaged is dissolved.
> If the king inlaws him, he comes back into the world like a new-born babe
> [Pollock and Maitland, 1898: Volume 1, 477; also see Volume 2, 580–581].

The condition of an excommunicate was similar, though not so extreme: "The excommunicate is . . . a spiritual leper; he can do no valid act in the law; he can not sue; but he can be sued [Pollock and Maitland, 1898: Volume 1, 478]." As late as the seventeenth century, an excommunicate still could not testify in an English court (Thomas, 1971:530), and other kinds of normative status also were known to have legal implications:

> The importance of neighbourly opinion was recognized by society as a
> whole. At ecclesiastical law a bad reputation ("ill fame") was sufficient to

justify a prosecution, while in the common law courts it was still accepted that the jury in a criminal trial were not impartial assessors, but members of the community from which the offender had sprung, and well-informed about his general standing in the community. When a Yorkshire gentleman had to stand trial for conspiracy in 1680 he demanded, and was granted, a jury composed of gentlemen of quality, from his own county, "that may be able to know something [of] how I have lived hitherto" [Thomas, 1971:528].

In modern societies, the "character witness" is brought to court for the same reason.

A known criminal is more vulnerable to law than a man without a record. He is more likely to be arrested, prosecuted, convicted, and punished. It is harder for him to get a parole from prison (see Sutherland, 1937: Chapter 5). For that matter, parole itself makes any ex-convict more vulnerable to law (see Irwin, 1970: Chapters 7–8). A man with a criminal record may also become subject to the specially severe punishment required by an "habitual criminal law" (see Sutherland and Cressey, 1960:563–564). A juvenile with a past record is more vulnerable as well:

If an officer decides he is dealing with a boy who is "guilty but essentially good" or "guilty but sometimes weak," the probability is high that he will decide to let the boy go with a warning about the consequences of committing this crime again . . . . On the other hand, if the officer decides that the offender is a "punk," a "persistent troublemaker," or some other version of a thoroughly bad boy, he may well decide to make an arrest . . . . The magnitude of an offense, of course, can become a factor in dispositions . . . . [But the] number of previous contacts with police has a more important effect on dispositions. These contacts are typically recorded on easily accessible files, and these files contain everything from arrests and convictions to contacts made on the flimsiest of contingent grounds. If a boy confesses to a crime and is not known to the police, he is often released. If he is caught for a third or fourth time, however, the sum total of previous contacts may be enough to affect a judgment about his moral character adversely, regardless of the nature or magnitude of the present offense and regardless of the reasons he was previously contacted [Werthman and Piliavin, 1967:72–73, italics omitted; see also Terry, 1967].

All motorcycle gangs and bohemians are disreputable to a degree, and so they are also more vulnerable to law (see Skolnick, 1966:94–96; Thompson, 1967; see also pages 69–73 of this volume). A man with a record of any kind is subject to suspicion (see Matza, 1969:180–197). He is more likely to be watched and harassed, and, if he deviates, it is worse. In fact, he is more likely to be defined as a deviant no matter what he does.

If a man with a record complains about someone who is more respectable, moreover, he is less likely to succeed. Like the outlaw in medieval England (see page 114), law may even leave him entirely without protection. In traditional India, for instance, a prostitute was so impure that it was permissible to kill her (Orenstein, 1968:126). In a modern society, some conduct toward a prostitute may be handled as crime, but it is still less serious than crime against more respectable people: The offender is less vulnerable to law, whether arrest, prosecution, conviction, or punishment. If killed in an accident, her life is worth less. In any lawsuit, she wins less. But then, like other disreputable people, she is less likely to complain anyway. Thus, the same applies to a prisoner, someone with a history of mental illness (see Lemert, 1962:15–16), or a pariah of any kind. Anyone who has been subject to social control has less protection, and any such person is more vulnerable to law as well.

*　*　*

The seriousness of deviant behavior corresponds to its direction and location in normative space. The most serious is a deviant act by an unrespectable party against a respectable party, followed by one between respectable people, then between unrespectable people; the least serious is a deviant act by a respectable against an unrespectable party. In this order comes law of every kind, whether a complaint, conviction, damages, or punishment. It might also be noted that among cases with the same normative direction—from more to less respectability or from less to more—deviant behavior is more serious if both parties are comparatively respectable than if both are comparatively unrespectable (see page 112). But this holds true only if the difference in respectability between the parties is constant.

*　*　*

A difference in respectability is a normative distance. This itself is a quantitative variable that predicts and explains law:

In a direction toward less respectability,
law varies directly with normative distance.

But:

In a direction toward more respectability,
law varies inversely with normative distance.

The less respectable an offender in relation to a complainant, a legal official, the members of a jury, or a witness, for instance, the more law to which he is likely to be subject. In other words, the more social control to which he has been subject before, the worse it is if he deviates again: Law varies inversely with the respectability of the offender. In modern America, for example, the longer and more recent the record of a man charged with drunkenness, the more likely he is to be sent to jail (Spradley, 1970:176–177; Wiseman, 1970:89–90; Mileski, 1971:504–505). This applies to legal matters of every kind. And it applies to the fate of a complainant as well: Law varies directly with the respectability of the victim. Any record of social control is a disadvantage, but a legal record is worse, especially a criminal record. And the worse it is, the worse yet it is likely to become.

LABELING AND DEVIANT BEHAVIOR

One theory of deviant behavior holds that the labeling of a deviant as such makes him more likely to deviate again. This is labeling theory. Each version of this theory has a different explanation of the deviant's motivation to deviate again (see, e.g., Lemert, 1967; Schur, 1971: Chapters 3–4). In one version, for instance, the explanation is the deprivation that comes with the deviant's loss of respectability, such as the difficulty of earning a living (see page 30). In another it is the marginality that he experiences, such as the loss of his former associates (see page 54), and in another it is the subculture of deviant behavior to which he is driven for support and protection (see page 79). Still another version explains this motivation with the deviant's reaction to social control itself, such as his sense of injustice (e.g., Matza, 1964: Chapter 4; Lemert, 1967:42–44) or his internalization of a deviant identity (e.g., Tannenbaum, 1938:17–22; Lofland, 1969: Chapters 7–8; Matza,

1969:157–180). In any event, every version of labeling theory holds that social control makes the deviant worse.

The facts show, indeed, that someone with a record of deviant behavior is more likely than others to deviate, and the longer and more serious his record, the more likely this is. In the United States, for instance, the majority of prisoners have been to a prison of some kind at least once before, and the majority of those released are convicted again (see, e.g., Sutherland and Cressey, 1960:482–483). Thus, a past offender is more likely than other people to get into trouble with the law, and this applies to arrest and prosecution as well as to conviction and sentencing. Labeling theory predicts this, explaining it with the principle that social control motivates the deviant to deviate again. Prison, for example, hardens the criminal, preparing him for a life of crime. And a prison record makes it more difficult to be a good citizen anyway.

The theory of law, however, predicts the same facts. But it explains these facts in a different way, without regard to the motivation or even the conduct of the deviant: Law is greater in a direction toward less respectability than toward more respectability. And, all else constant, law varies inversely with the respectability of the offender (see pages 114, 117). Hence, someone who has been in trouble before is more likely to get into trouble again, no matter what he does. And the worse his record is, the more is this the case. He is more likely, for instance, to be the subject of surveillance, a complaint, a search of his person or premises, an arrest, a prosecution, a conviction, or a severe sentence. Moreover, the conduct of a past offender is more likely to be defined as illegal in the first place. In effect, he is on parole all of his life, always subject to revocation. And the longer and more serious his record, the more likely he is to fall further into disrepute. In this sense, then, social control makes the deviant worse, but regardless of his motivation or conduct.

THE BEHAVIOR OF SOCIAL CONTROL

It is possible to explain social control of every kind with other normative life. Like law, each kind of social control varies with other kinds, and each varies with its own normative location and direction. This applies to every style of social control, whether penal, compensatory, therapeutic, or conciliatory. Consider, for example, the treatment of mental illness.

Whether known as madness, magical fright, or mental illness, conduct defined and treated as abnormal is subject to many kinds of social control. This includes social control within a family, among friends, and in a workplace, neighborhood, or village. The more of this to which a person is subject, the less likely is a definition of his conduct as mad or sick and the less likely is psychiatric care or other treatment by a specialist. In other words: The treatment of mental illness varies inversely with other social control. In modern society, for instance, psychiatric care varies inversely with family control. Thus, someone who lives alone is more likely than someone in a family to seek the help of a psychiatrist. Others, including the psychiatrist, are also more likely to define him as mentally ill. He is more likely to be hospitalized, to stay longer, and, if released, to be rehospitalized (see, e.g., Dinitz, Lefton, Angrist, and Pasamanick, 1961:327). And the weaker the social control in a family, the more likely are its members to be defined and treated as mentally ill (see Horwitz, 1975). But one member may be subject to more family control than another, and so he would have more immunity. A child, for example, can do almost anything without being called crazy, and he is less likely to find himself in a mental hospital. The same applies to someone subject to more social control in other settings, such as among his friends or workmates. In this sense, mental illness varies with its setting. And the less social control of other kinds that is available, the worse it is.

The same principle explains the treatment of mental illness across history and societies. The invention and growth of the mental hospital, for instance, came with the breakdown of kinship and other kinds of social control. The modern family expels its abnormal members (see Aubert, 1958:72–73), and it is more likely to regard them as abnormal in the first place. In societies where family control is still strong, however, madmen are kept at home. In rural Ghana, for example, mental hospitals are available but are rarely used, even for cases that are extremely serious from a modern standpoint:

> The majority of chronic schizophrenics in rural districts are treated with such patient and sustained kindness by their relatives and tolerance by their neighbors that the prognosis for their recovery is probably better than it would be were they herded with other patients in understaffed mental hospitals. If they have phases of destructive violence or of wandering off into the bush they are usually locked up or fettered to a log during these phases but are released at the earliest moment . . . . The younger schizophrenics are always cared for by their parents, the mothers especially displaying impressively uncomplaining devotion. After the parents' death the brothers and sisters take over [Field, 1960:453–454].

The Zapotec Indians of Mexico also absorb people who would be hospitalized as mentally ill in a more modern setting:

> Crazy people ate, drank, and socialized with everyone else . . . . One man regularly went into psychotic states and equally regularly emerged from them, but the villagers were not interested in his condition. Another man had to be restrained within the house, if barring the door of a bamboo hut can be called restraint . . . . Practically speaking, there were no culturally defined psychotics in the community, although there were certainly people we would define as psychotic [Selby, 1974:41–42, punctuation edited].

A traditional family has its own social control for its own members. By contrast, a modern family has less of this and is even likely to be the first to suggest that its own member seek professional help (see Clausen and Yarrow, 1955:28; Goffman, 1959a:133–139). If the family continues to weaken across the world, then, more and more people will be defined as mentally ill and treated in mental hospitals.

The treatment of mental illness varies with its normative location and direction as well. Thus, like law, it varies directly with respectability. Respectable people hold each other to higher standards of mental health than do unrespectable people. In a modern society, for instance, reputable citizens such as businessmen or professionals are more likely to define each other as mentally ill than are people with less normative status, such as prostitutes, drug addicts, or prisoners. Respectable people are more likely to speak of one another as neurotic or alcoholic, for example, to define themselves in this way, and to seek the help of a psychiatrist.

The treatment of mental illness may also have a direction in normative space, and, like law, it is greater toward less respectability than toward more. This means that someone with a past record of deviant behavior is more likely to be defined as mentally ill by a more respectable person than vice versa. A history of mental illness is itself such a record, and so an ex-mental patient is more likely than others to be defined and treated as mentally ill (compare Gove, 1970). He is also more likely to define himself in this way. In fact, in modern America, one-third of those released from mental hospitals are readmitted (Goffman, 1959a:131, note 5). If an ex-mental patient or other ex-deviant calls someone else crazy, however, people are less likely to listen. And the longer his record is, and the more respectable those around him, the greater are these differences. In other words, in a direction toward less respectability, the treatment of mental illness varies directly with normative distance; and, in the opposite direction, it varies inversely with normative distance.

In the mental hospital itself the patient's record, or case history, is readily available for reference, detailing everything deviant that he has ever done (see Goffman, 1959a:155–165). And the worse this record is, the harder it is for him to get out. The length of his treatment itself enters his case history, measuring the seriousness of his illness, and so the longer he is hospitalized, the less likely is his release (see Scheff, 1966:165–167). In this sense, then, the treatment of mental illness makes it worse and worse.

7

ANARCHY

Anarchy is social life without law, that is, without governmental social control (see page 2). It is a quantitative variable, the inverse of law. Like law, then, the quantity of anarchy varies across societies, across the settings of a single society, and across time. An entire society may be anarchic, with no law at all from day to day, or some of its settings may be anarchic and not others. In tribal Africa, for example, many entire societies were anarchic, such as the Arusha and Ndendeuli of what is now Tanzania (Gulliver, 1963; 1969), the Logoli and Vugusu of Kenya (Wagner, 1940), the Lugbara and Amba of Uganda (Middleton, 1956; 1958; Winter, 1958), the Nuer of the Sudan (Evans-Pritchard, 1940a; 1940b), the Bedouin of Cyrenaica (Peters, 1967), the Tallensi of Ghana (Fortes, 1940), the Tiv of Nigeria (Bohannan, 1957), and the Tonga of Zambia (Colson, 1953). Anarchic societies in other parts of the world included the Ifugao of the Philippines (Barton, 1919), the Aborigines of Australia (Meggitt, 1962: Chapter 14), the Tangu and Kapauku of New Guinea (Burridge, 1957; Pospisil, 1958), the Yaps of Micronesia (Schneider, 1957), the Jibaros of Equador and Peru (Karsten, 1923), the Carib of Guyana (Gillin, 1934), and most of the Indians and Eskimos of North America

(Lantis, 1946; Lowie, 1948; Hoebel, 1954: Chapters 5, 7). An anarchic society may have an occasional episode of law, such as during a war, hunt, or migration (see pages 87–91), but it has other kinds of social control in its everyday life.

The earliest societies were anarchic (see, e.g., Service, 1971). Hence, law is an historical phenomenon, not universal, whereas anarchy is found in all societies to some degree. In a modern society, for example, much anarchy appears in the social life of children, among friends and colleagues, within families and subcultures, among transients, isolates, disreputables, and others on the edges of social life, and also between people separated by great distances in social space, foreigners of all kinds. Much appears among nations as well.

Since anarchy is social life without law, principles that predict and explain the quantity of law also predict and explain, by implication, the quantity of anarchy. Just as it is possible to predict and explain law from variable aspects of stratification, morphology, culture, organization, and social control (as in Chapters 2–6), so these predict and explain anarchy. The conditions favorable to anarchy are opposite those favorable to law: Since the relationship between law and stratification is direct, for example (see page 13), between anarchy and stratification it is inverse. Since the relationship between law and differentiation is curvilinear (see page 39), between anarchy and differentiation it is ∪-curvilinear. Notice that the conditions favorable to law are mutually compatible, so that it is possible to imagine them all in a single setting. One setting might have, for example, much stratification; moderate differentiation, relational distance, and cultural distance; much culture and organization; and little social control other than law—all conditions favorable to law (Chapters 2–6). Several of the conditions favorable to anarchy, however, appear to be mutually antithetical. In particular, where the relationship between law and other social life is curvilinear, anarchy is most likely at the extremes, under opposite conditions. This applies to the relationship between law and differentiation (see page 39), law and relational distance (see page 41), and law and cultural distance (see page 74). Anarchy thus is more likely where people are either symbiotic or independent, and either close or distant, but it is less likely between these extremes. Moreover, in all known societies these extremes have appeared in different settings, and different kinds of anarchy have corresponded to each.

TWO KINDS OF ANARCHY

One kind of anarchy appears where people are equal, symbiotic, intimate, homogeneous, and unorganized. In other words, it is found in a world of closeness, similarity, and stability. This is communal anarchy. A second kind appears where people are again equal and unorganized, but where they are independent of one another instead of symbiotic, complete strangers instead of intimates, and heterogeneous instead of homogeneous. It is found in a world of distance, diversity, and change. This is situational anarchy. Thus, each kind of anarchy is found under opposite conditions. And yet each appears to some degree in the life of nearly every society.

Consider a simple society such as a tribe of hunters and gatherers or herdsmen (see Service, 1971: Chapters 3–4). In the pure case of this kind, man knows only two social worlds, each the opposite of the other. At one extreme are his own people, those of his everyday life, people like himself—his "little community" (see Redfield, 1955). He knows everyone else, since each is a neighbor if not a kinsman. At another extreme, however, are the people on the periphery of his life, those of foreign societies, complete strangers rarely seen. If he encounters people of this kind, it is only a momentary transaction without a future. In a simple society, then, life polarizes between the close and the distant, the familiar and the strange, the permanent and the temporary. At each extreme is anarchy, but a different kind at each. Communal anarchy appears in the family, camp, or village, situational anarchy between foreigners. And there is nothing else. Although pure cases such as this appeared in times past, the degree of polarization varies considerably. In some societies the transition from the familiar to the foreign is sudden and complete, without gradations between the extremes, as in the pure case. But in others this transition is more gradual, with some camps or villages nearby, still others further away, with kinsmen in some and not in others. A tribe may also have routine contact with foreigners, as in a trade or other exchange relationship. But all simple people live most of their lives among intimates. And for all of them, most strangers are complete strangers. Even if the degree varies, therefore, polarization appears in the social life of every simple society, and at each pole is anarchy.

In a modern society, by contrast, life does not polarize between extremes of this kind. Most is intermediate, neither very close nor very distant, neither familiar nor completely strange. Life in the market, for example, is neither intimate nor alien, but between, impersonal and yet routine. Modern life is a spectrum of settings, with inequality in some and not in others, networks and subcultures of diverse kinds, and all manner of groups and organizations. Social control is everywhere, one jurisdiction sometimes conflicting with another, one style conflicting with the next. Many of these settings have law; but at the extremes are settings similar to those of a simple society, and these have anarchy, some communal, others situational. At one extreme are settings where life is close and stable, such as within families and friendships, among peers and neighbors. No matter how modern a society may be in other respects, it still has residues of tribal life, of equality, intimacy, sameness, permanence. And here law rarely appears; these are the settings of communal anarchy in modern life. At another extreme are settings where life is mobile and people very distant from one another, complete strangers, in contact only for the moment. This is life on a transcontinental highway, a metropolitan sidewalk, or wherever foreigners meet. These are the settings of situational anarchy in modern life; they might as well be encounters between strange tribes in the bush, thousands of years ago.

SOCIAL CONTROL IN ANARCHIC SETTINGS

Anarchy has its own kinds of social control. Whether tribal or modern, moreover, the same kinds of settings have the same kinds of social control. First, consider the intimate settings of a simple society, the world of communal anarchy. Here social control ranges from banishment and beating to ridicule and teasing. Murder might be repaid in kind, for instance, or nearly ignored. Thus, among the Bedouin of Cyrenaica, the killer of a close relative might only be labeled with an epithet such as "one who defecates in the tent" (Peters, 1967:264). Among the Lugbara of Uganda, a man who killed his brother was avoided as unnatural, but he was subject to no other action (Middleton, 1965:51). In traditional Albania, a son who killed his father was stigmatized as a bastard, since a natural son could not conceivably do this (Hasluck, 1954:210–211), a pattern also found among the Bedouin (Peters, 1967:275). In other simple societies, banishment or assassination might arise in response to a single instance of an offense such as murder, but more often would be imposed only after a series of offenses:

> What elicits the sanction of banishment most surely is a long succession of social mistakes and misdeeds which in cumulation indicate a person unfit for society. Sometimes, banishment of such a person comes after he finally commits a serious offense. More often, it follows a minor delict which the society or social unit receives as a "last straw" [Baumgartner, 1974:2–3].

Among the Barama River Carib of British Guiana (now Guyana), for instance:

> Only in cases . . . in which an individual by the multiplicity and pertinacity of his offenses makes himself a public nuisance or a public menace do the members of the group take united action against him. And in such cases it appears that the group action is taken as the result of a sum of individual grievances rather than from a conscious sociological consideration for the welfare of the group as an entity [Gillin, 1934:334].

Banishment and assassination define the "finally intolerable" (Llewellyn and Hoebel, 1941:49, note 5; see also Hoebel, 1954:88–90; Westermeyer, 1973a:125–127; 1973b:741), each being a way to separate the otherwise inseparable. In many simple societies the same applies to an accusation of witchcraft: Coming after a series of minor offenses and annoyances, it blasts apart a relationship that would otherwise continue indefinitely (see Marwick, 1970:380; Mitchell, 1965; Swartz, 1969). Among other kinds of social control in intimate societies are revenge, compensation, and voluntary exile. Still another is suicide, either by the offender (e.g., Hoebel, 1954:161) or by the offended (see Jeffreys, 1952). In many societies, suicide by an offended party could even result in the labeling of the offender as a murderer (e.g., Llewellyn and Hoebel, 1941:160–161; Jeffreys, 1952:120–121). Finally, where people are divided into similar segments, themselves contiguous, another possibility is the feud.

When a feud or other dispute arises within the tribe, a third party may step forth in the role of mediator, much as an adult or older sibling may mediate a dispute between children. Among the Ifugao of the Philippines, for example, this was the function of the *monkalun:*

> The *monkalun* is a whole court, completely equipped, in embryo. He is judge, prosecuting and defending counsel, and the court record . . . . To the end of peaceful settlement he exhausts every art of Ifugao diplomacy. He wheedles, coaxes, flatters, threatens, drives, scolds, insinuates. He beats down the demands of the plaintiffs or prosecution, and bolsters up the proposals of the defendants until a point be reached at which the two parties may compromise . . . . The *monkalun* has no authority. All that he can do is to act as a peace making go-between. His only power is in his art of persuasion, his tact and his skillful playing on human emotions and motives [Barton, 1919:87].

Among the Nuer of the Sudan, the "leopard-skin chief" was a mediator of the same kind:

> The leopard-skin chief does not rule and judge, but acts as a mediator through whom communities desirous of ending open hostility can conclude an active state of feud . . . . [He] may also act as mediator in disputes concerning ownership of cattle, and he and the elders on both sides may express their opinion on the merits of a case. But the chief does not summon the defendants, for he has neither court nor jurisdiction and, moreover, has no means of compelling compliance. All he can do is to go with the plaintiff and some elders of his community to the home of the defendant and to ask him and his kinsmen to discuss the matter . . . . In the strict sense of the word, the Nuer have no law [Evans-Pritchard, 1940b:293; see also Greuel, 1971].

And a similar pattern appeared among the Navajo Indians of North America, a tradition still alive to some degree:

> There is no formal mechanism for handling disputes. The persons most directly concerned, usually members of the immediate families, take the initiative in calling a meeting of interested parties to which they invite some

local influentials, chosen for wisdom and diplomacy to act as mediators. The mediator has no authority to intervene or to force a decision . . . . Verbal pressure will be brought by all those present upon the disputants to compromise their differences or to agree on restitution for injury. A very powerful ideal in Navajo society is the plea to "shake hands and forget all about it" [Shepardson, 1965:251].

In other societies an informal court, a moot or conclave, would convene for the same purpose (see, e.g., Bohannan, 1957: Chapter 9; Gulliver, 1963:121–127; 1969). Whether an individual or a group, however, the third party typically is more an agent of compromise than of judgment. In general, then, social control in a tribal society is more remedial than accusatory (see pages 4–5). Only occasionally is a relationship torn apart, as in banishment, assassination, or suicide. A relationship continues, even with a killer, or it ends completely.

In a modern society, intimate settings have social control much like that of a tribal society. In a family, friendship, or romantic couple, in a fraternity or among playmates, social control typically protects the life of relationships. Modern intimates tease, admonish, and beat each other, but they have ways of "making up," such as apologizing, gift giving, or hand shaking. And when they have a feud or other dispute, a third party may help with a reconciliation, much like a mediator in a tribal society. But occasionally, often after a long series of offenses, destruction may result as well: banishment, such as disowning or "blackballing"; ostracism, such as the "cold shoulder"; divorce or "breaking up"; voluntary exile; even assassination or suicide. But a modern assassination is likely, in turn, to result in legal action, even if it is a kind of social control when and where it happens. Similarly, only those close to a suicide may recognize it as an instance of social control; they may accept it as the self-punishment of an offender or, on the other hand, blame someone for it, as if he were a murderer. In any event, wherever social life is intimate, homogeneous, and stable, whether in a tribal or a modern setting, the patterns of social control are comparable. Communal anarchy appears under the same conditions everywhere.

This applies to situational anarchy as well. Social control in encounters between tribes or other strangers is primitive and ephemeral. Its jurisdiction is temporary, its sovereignty for the moment only, with no lasting relationship to repair or destroy, nothing to reconcile or separate. Instead, one party may threaten or coerce the other with brute force, or he may do nothing more than glare or posture, defining the other as the deviant of the situation. Or a struggle over who is deviant may arise, in turn resulting in mutual staring or even a fight. In any event, if social control happens at all, it is sudden, possibly crude, and always finished quickly. For tribal people, experiences of this kind are infrequent. In a modern society, however, a similar pattern is found in encounters between strangers in public places, for many people an aspect of everyday life:

> The individual finds himself not so much with a guide for action (although presumably on occasion there is that), but a guide as to what to be alive to, a guide that tells him what is seeable in a particular situation and therefore what it is to which he might be well advised to take a stand—whether to offer an account, an apology, an excuse, whether to mock or guy, whether to bluster through uncaringly . . . . The complete cycle of crime, apprehension, trial, punishment, and return to society can run its course in two gestures and a glance. Justice is summary . . . . Thus, social situations are not to be seen as places where rules are obeyed or secretly broken, but rather as settings for racing through versions in miniature of the entire judicial process [Goffman, 1971:185, 107; see also Lofland, 1973: Chapter 5].

In modern America, for example, members of juvenile gangs may hold brief skirmishes with strangers who unwittingly enter their streetcorner "hangout":

> Gang members communicate their claims on the hangout by calling an abrupt halt to verbal interchange in such a way as to suggest that a legitimate setting for private conversation has been rudely intruded upon. The members may begin to stare, and out of the hostile silence may come a wisecrack or taunt. The boys are usually willing to accept a noticeable increase in walking pace and lowered eyes as sufficient implicit apology. [A stranger] who continues to behave impolitely, either by refusing to hurry out of the space or by challenging the reality offered to him by the boys, becomes eligible for sanctions otherwise appropriate to a common housebreaker [Werthman and Piliavin, 1967:60].

This is not to deny that such conduct on a public sidewalk may also attract the attention of the police (see Werthman and Piliavin, 1967:61–62). For that matter, many settings once largely anarchic have increasingly become subject to law.

THE EVOLUTION OF LAW

Over history, across the world, law has been increasing. This also means that the rate of crime and other illegality has been increasing, since this is defined by law itself (compare Erikson, 1966: Chapter 4). The growth of law has continued over the centuries, despite lesser declines from time to time. Moreover, it is possible to explain the evolution of law with other trends in social life. Beginning with the earliest and simplest societies, these trends have included the following: Stratification, or inequality of wealth, has generally increased. Differentiation has increased. The quantity and diversity of culture have increased, and yet at the same time the extreme diversity once seen across societies has been decreasing. The organization of social life has increased, but members of groups have become more autonomous as well. On the other hand, intimacy has decreased, even with a lesser countertrend of increasing intimacy across people once entirely isolated from one another. Finally, social control other than law has decreased. Since the evolution of law obeys the same principles as any other kind of legal variation (see Chapters 2–6), these trends explain the increase of law over the centuries.

If these trends continue into the future, law will increase all the more. If the history of the modern world repeats itself in the simpler societies—for instance, in Africa, Asia, Oceania, and Latin America—inequality will increase in these areas, as will differentiation, the quantity and diversity of culture, and organization. People will mingle with an increasing number of strangers. Nevertheless, the extreme relational and cultural distances long separating different peoples will narrow at the same time. And traditional social control will wither away still more. As all of this happens, law will increase; and, if all of these trends continue in the modern world, it will increase to a level never before imagined. This applies to social life among nations as well. If the division of labor among nations continues to increase, for example, international law will increase.

Everywhere, law increases with the evolution from tribal to modern life, status to contract (Maine, 1861:163–165), *Gemeinschaft* to *Gesellschaft* (Tönnies, 1887), from mechanical to organic solidarity

(Durkheim, 1893), from folk to urban society (Redfield, 1947). If all of this continues, anarchy will decline to its lowest level in history. But if some of these trends continue into the future, and if countertrends now only dimly visible continue until they dominate some of these older trends, a point will come at which law no longer increases. A point will come at which law even begins to decline. This has already happened in some settings: Statutes have been repealed, penalties reduced, surveillance ended. In short, if the evolution of social life continues on its present course, into the indefinite future, anarchy will return (compare Engels, 1878:306–307).

THE RETURN OF ANARCHY

Over the centuries, social life has been drifting in two great patterns. On the one hand, the intimate life of earlier times has been coming apart. On the other hand, what was separate has been drawing together. Thus, social life has been moving away from the extremes of communal and situational life, the conditions of anarchy. All this time, law has been increasing. If these drifts continue, however, social life will evolve into something new, neither communal nor situational as before, but a synthesis of the two. It will have characteristics of each, but it will be different from both. Imagine, in one setting, closeness and distance, similarity and diversity, stability and change. Imagine people who are symbiotic and yet interchangeable, intimate and homogeneous in some respects, strangers and heterogeneous in others; imagine organizations with a constant circulation of members, and imagine a constant circulation of advantage and reputation, with inequality and stigmatization, if any, only temporary. If trends of the past continue, and countertrends, settings of this kind will appear. If this happens, moreover, aspects of the past will return, but social life will be new at the same time.

First consider stratification. The earliest societies, simple tribes, had little inequality of wealth. Modern life has much, and in some respects this is still increasing. Nevertheless, a countertrend of equalization has begun (see Tocqueville, 1835; Bell, 1974:24–25; Paglin, 1975). Consider, for example, the history of property such as land and other real estate. The earliest societies had communal ownership (see Morgan, 1877:447). Who could use what land in what way was a matter of mutual understanding. Among settled people, these understandings were traditional; among nomads, they were temporary. The distribution was largely equal, as was the distribution of dwellings. Individual ownership and the right of transfer emerged only slowly, over centuries, and only as this happened did inequality in real estate come into being. During an intermediate period, ownership of land was vested in families, as in ancient Greece, Rome, and India, but for a long time a family had no right to transfer its ownership to others (Fustel de Coulanges, 1864:70–71). Individual ownership and the right of transfer reached their peak in the nineteenth century, and since then a reversal has been taking place. Although inequality has continued, less and less have people been able to do with their land or other real estate what they choose. In some societies, this is a result of zoning laws, housing and building codes, environmental protection laws, and other public claims on private property (see Rudel, 1973). In others, it is a result of the abolition of private ownership of land and most other real estate. If this trend continues across the world, the history of ownership will be circular, ending with the communal ownership, and equality, of the past (see Engels, 1884). Once again, who uses what real estate in what way will be a matter of understanding. And, with the increasing mobility of modern life, these understandings will be temporary, not a matter of tradition. Inequality, if any, will be temporary, as among nomads.

Other trends of this kind include the increasing equalization of social classes, races, sexes, and ages. Dependents of all kinds—slaves, wives, children—have gained rights. Once property, they have become, to some degree, persons. It might be noted that, even if the earliest societies had equality in most other respects, they did not have equality between the ages, but if the trend continues, this will come as well (see Dresch, 1973:17–18). Hence, the future may have even more equality than the distant past. In any event, the earliest societies had little stratification, and the future may have little again.

Increasing differentiation is another trend of modern life (see, e.g., Parsons, 1966). This implies increasing interdependence across social life, with one part increasingly depending on another, one role on another. Industry is increasingly specialized, for example, so that the product of one factory, or the job of one worker, is useless by itself. Note, however, that differentiation of this kind, or functional differentiation, does not imply differences across people as such, or personal differentiation. Rather, even though one person may be identical to another in his skills and other characteristics, each may have a different role in the division of labor; and the same applies to organizations and other groups. People may thus depend upon one another even though they are similar in most respects, since they depend upon a function, not upon a person or group as such. The people themselves may even be interchangeable. In fact, interchangeability of this kind is a trend of modern life.

With the automation of production, for instance, the skilled worker disappears, as did the craftsman before him. Each job makes a different contribution, and yet one can do the jobs of all. It does not even matter what the product is. Increasingly, factories and other systems of production are interchangeable as well, able to move from one product to another. As in production, so in distribution, one job is increasingly the same as the next. And yet all this time differentiation itself increases. More and more, then, a person depends upon others for his survival, and yet, individually, one person is the same as the next. This combination of differentiation and interchangeability has never been seen before. Even though differentiation of this degree would be new, however, interchangeability would be a return to the past. In the earliest societies, the people of each sex were much the same, with the same skills and the same functions. But even though they were not specialized, they were interdependent to a degree. Adding the work of one to another, in a multiplication of labor, they had strength in numbers.

It should also be noted that in the simple societies of the past, changing places with another implied little or no mobility across physical space. One work setting was close to the next. In modern life, by contrast, a great distance may separate one work setting from another. What is more, increasingly people are changing places across these distances. The rate of horizontal mobility is increasing (see Sorokin, 1927: Chapter 16). More and more, people circulate from one setting to another and one role to another. Increasingly, they circulate from city to city, region to region, nation to nation. Other kinds of circulation have been increasing as well, such as movement from one residence to another and, with modern transportation, from one neighborhood or city to another, day by day, even hour by hour. All of this is a return to the nomadic life of the earliest societies, the hunters and gatherers (Sorokin, 1927:382). But the early nomad moved with his fellow tribesmen, whereas the modern nomad abandons and renews social relationships as he moves from place to place. He is a nomad without a tribe.

Now consider the history of intimacy. Traditional ties have been loosening, even falling apart altogether. The community is weaker than ever before, and so is the neighborhood and family. The life span of relationships grows shorter and shorter. Increasingly, marriage does not last, for instance, and friends fluctuate from month to month, if not from week to week or day to day. Encounters replace the social structures of the past, and people increasingly have closeness without permanence, depth without commitment. In the old days, intimacy was communal, but now it is becoming situational. The family is still intimate, and the friendship, but here and there intimacy appears between strangers—between fellow travelers, in a café, in transitory meetings of all kinds. It becomes possible to relate as openly and deeply to a stranger as to a neighbor or friend or spouse. As communal life of the old kind deteriorates, this happens more and more.

But the history of intimacy has another aspect. Even as the older ties come undone, new ones appear where none had been before. Over the centuries, the number of societies has been decreasing, one merging into another, each embracing ever more people. If this continues, a single society will eventually cover the whole world (see Wallas, 1914: Chapter 1). Each person, on his own, ventures into social life, meeting others who once were foreigners. But a world society has no foreigners. It is a great tribe, but everything is temporary; everything is familiar and yet changing constantly, close and distant at the same time.

Culture, too, has been drifting into a new configuration. Old styles of life have increasingly come into contact with one another, losing their purity. From the standpoint of a single culture, this is diversification, but from the standpoint of the world, it is homogenization. If this continues, the number of cultural patterns will grow steadily smaller until, eventually, only one is left. As this happens, much culture will die out, never to be seen again in its natural setting. Many languages are dead already, for example, and, if the trend continues, eventually only one will remain. Many religions are losing their believers, decorations their designers, arts their artists. If these trends continue, the culture of the world will become homogeneous, then, like the culture of a tribe. But it will change constantly, diversifying across situations instead of across societies.

Another trend is the increasing organization of social life. This applies to private as well as public life, to business, education, science, and government. Decision making is ever more centralized, cooperation ever more a part of everyday life. Even as this happens, however, the scope of organization—the degree to which a group incorporates its members—has begun to decrease. At one extreme, broad in scope, is an organization that encapsulates all of a member's activities, every day, all day, for his entire life, such as a prison or monastery (see Goffman, 1961a). At the other extreme is an organization that touches only a single moment of a member's life, as in a business transaction or a door-to-door survey. Even as organization increases in many respects, its scope has begun to drift in the opposite direction. Increasingly, people circulate from one organization to another. The organizations live on, but the life span of membership grows shorter and shorter. Even day by day, the hours given by each member shorten as well. Less and less do people give their lives to organizations; in their conduct, they have less and less loyalty. As the scope of organization shortens in time, it also narrows in focus. Members of all kinds have begun to rebel against their organizations, demanding and receiving rights they never had (see Selznick, 1969: Chapter 7). Just as citizens gain more rights from the state, students gain more from their schools, employees from corporations, soldiers from the military, inmates from prisons. Accordingly, privacy is increasing, and subordination has begun to decline. Increasingly, organization is becoming a tool of the membership and nothing more (compare Marcuse, 1955: Chapters 2–4, 6, 10). In the simple societies of the past, people organized for war or a hunt, even

to the point of dictatorship, surrendering their usual liberties for the
time. Organization was temporary but strong (see pages 87–91).
In the future, if trends continue, it will be permanent but weak.
People may again live most of their lives without it.

Now, finally, consider the future of social control. If trends
continue, social control will decrease to some degree, but old patterns
will reappear in new locations, with a new significance. Banishment
will still be possible, for instance, but only banishment from an
encounter, not from home. The intolerable becomes, at most, situational. Similarly, as people increasingly move, alone, from location
to location, social control loses its fatefulness. With people constantly
moving, and constantly making and losing friends and enemies, the
life span of disputes shortens, feuding becomes difficult if not impossible, and mediators and tribunals of all kinds lose their importance. And if a relationship does not last, neither does a reputation
won or lost in it. Accordingly, normative mobility, in and out of
respectability, increases as much as other mobility. Already a rebel-
lion against dossiers and other records has begun (see Wheeler,
1969). If this continues, disgrace will become only temporary, and
people will have nothing left to hide. In a world of this kind, as in
simple societies of the past, social control will mend relationships
completely, or completely tear them apart. But, in any case, situations
will be all that matter, all that are saved or destroyed.

* * *

If all of these trends continue, a new society will come into
being, possibly centuries from now, possibly sooner. It will be a
society of equals, people specialized and yet interchangeable; a society of nomads, at once close and distant, homogeneous and diverse,
organized and autonomous, where reputations and other statuses
fluctuate from one day to the next. The past will return to some
degree, yet society will be different. It will be communal and situational at the same time, a unity of opposites, a situational society. To
some degree, moreover, anarchy will return. But it will be a new
anarchy, as new as society itself, neither communal nor situational,
and yet both at once. If these trends continue, then, law will decrease. It might even disappear.

REFERENCES

Adams, Robert McC.
  1966 *The Evolution of Urban Society: Early Mesopotamia and Prehispanic Mexico.* Chicago: Aldine.
  1972 "Demography and the 'urban revolution' in lowland Mesopotamia." Pages 60–63 in *Population Growth: Anthropological Implications,* edited by Brian Spooner. Cambridge: M.I.T. Press.
Andenaes, Johannes
  1966 "The general preventive effects of punishment." *University of Pennsylvania Law Review* 114 (May): 949–983.
Anderson, Nels
  1923 *The Hobo: The Sociology of the Homeless Man.* Chicago: University of Chicago Press.
Arendt, Hannah
  1958 *The Origins of Totalitarianism.* Cleveland: World Publishing Company (second edition; first edition, 1951).
Asbury, Herbert
  1928 *The Gangs of New York: An Informal History of the Underworld.* Garden City: Garden City Publishing Company.
Aubert, Vilhelm
  1958 "Legal justice and mental health." Pages 55–82 in *The Hidden Society.* Totowa: Bedminster Press, 1965.
Aubert, Vilhelm, and Sheldon L. Messinger
  1958 "The criminal and the sick." Pages 25–54 in *The Hidden Society,* by V. Aubert. Totowa: Bedminster Press, 1965.
Aubert, Vilhelm, and Harrison White
  1959 "Sleep: a sociological interpretation." Pages 168–200 in *The Hidden Society,* by V. Aubert. Totowa: Bedminster Press, 1965.
Bacon, Selden D.
  1939 The Early Development of American Municipal Police: A Study of the Evolution of Formal Controls in a Changing Society. Unpublished doctoral dissertation, Department of Political Science, Yale University.
Banton, Michael
  1964 *The Policeman in the Community.* London: Tavistock.
Barber, Bernard
  1961 "Resistance by scientists to scientific discovery." *Science* 134 (September 1):596–602.
Barkun, Michael
  1968 *Law without Sanctions: Order in Primitive Societies and the World Community.* New Haven: Yale University Press.
Barnard, Chester I.
  1946 "Functions and pathology of status systems in formal organizations." Pages 207–244 in *Organization and Management: Selected Papers.* Cambridge: Harvard University Press, 1956.
Barth, Fredrik
  1961 *Nomads of South Persia: The Basseri Tribe of the Khamseh Confederacy.* Boston: Little, Brown.

Barton, Roy Franklin
    1919   *Ifugao Law.* Berkeley: University of California Press, 1969.
    1949   "A comparison of the present world situation with the Kalinga state."
            Unpublished paper, Department of Anthropology, University of Chicago.
Baumgartner, M.P.
    1972   "A Puritan court: the response to capital crime in colonial New Haven."
            Unpublished paper, Department of Sociology, Yale University.
    1973   "Capital punishment and the morphology of government." Unpublished
            paper, Department of Sociology, Yale University.
    1974   "Patterns of banishment." Unpublished paper, Department of Sociology,
            Yale University.
    1975   Law and Social Status in Colonial New Haven, 1639–1665. Unpublished
            senior essay, Department of Sociology, Yale University.
Baxter, P.T.W.
    1972   "Absence makes the heart grow fonder: some suggestions why witch-
            craft accusations are rare among East African pastoralists." Pages 163–
            191 in *The Allocation of Responsibility*, edited by Max Gluckman. Man-
            chester: Manchester University Press.
Beattie, J.H.M.
    1957   "Informal judicial activity in Bunyoro." *Journal of African Administration* 9
            (October):188–195.
Becker, Howard S.
    1963   *Outsiders: Studies in the Sociology of Deviance.* New York: Free Press.
    1974   "Art as collective action." *American Sociological Review* 39 (Dec.):767–776.
Beidelman, T.O.
    1966   "Intertribal tensions in some local government courts in colonial Tan-
            ganyika: I." *Journal of African Law* 10 (Summer):118–130.
    1967   "Intertribal tensions in some local government courts in colonial Tan-
            ganyika: II." *Journal of African Law* 11 (Spring):27–45.
Bell, Wendell
    1974   "A conceptual analysis of equality and equity in evolutionary perspec-
            tive." *American Behavioral Scientist* 18 (September):8–35.
Ben-David, Joseph
    1971   *The Scientist's Role in Society: A Comparative Study.* Englewood Cliffs:
            Prentice-Hall.
Bendix, Reinhard, and Seymour Martin Lipset (editors)
    1953   *Class, Status and Power: A Reader in Social Stratification.* New York: Free
            Press.
Benedict, Ruth
    1934   *Patterns of Culture.* New York: New American Library, 1946.
Berger, Peter L., and Hansfried Kellner
    1964   "Marriage and the construction of reality: an exercise in the microsociol-
            ogy of knowledge." *Diogenes* 46 (Spring):1–25.
Berman, Harold J.
    1963   *Justice in the U.S.S.R.: An Interpretation of Soviet Law.* New York: Random
            House (second edition; first edition, 1950).
Berman, Jesse
    1969   "The Cuban popular tribunals." *Columbia Law Review* 69
            (December):1317–1354.

Black, Donald
  1970   "Production of crime rates." *American Sociological Review* 35
         (August):733–748.
  1971   "The social organization of arrest." *Stanford Law Review* 23 (June):1087–
         1111.
  1972   "The boundaries of legal sociology." *Yale Law Journal* 81 (May):1086–
         1100.
Blake, Judith, and Kingsley Davis
  1964   "Norms, values, and sanctions." Pages 456–484 in *Handbook of Modern
         Sociology,* edited by Robert E.L. Faris. Chicago: Rand McNally.
Blau, Peter M.
  1970   "A formal theory of differentiation in organizations." *American Sociologi-
         cal Review* 35 (April):201–218.
Block, Richard
  1974   "Why notify the police: the victim's decision to notify the police of an
         assault." *Criminology* 11 (February):555–569.
Blumstein, Philip W. (with the assistance of nine collaborators)
  1974   "The honoring of accounts." *American Sociological Review* 39
         (August):551–566.
Bohannan, Paul
  1957   *Justice and Judgment among the Tiv.* London: Oxford University Press.
  1965   "The differing realms of the law." Pages 33–42 in *The Ethnography of
         Law,* edited by Laura Nader. Published as supplement to *American An-
         thropologist,* Volume 67, December.
  1968   "Law and legal institutions." Pages 73–78 in *International Encyclopedia of
         the Social Sciences,* edited by David L. Sills. New York: Free Press.
         Volume 9.
Bonger, William Adrian
  1916   *Criminality and Economic Conditions.* Boston: Little, Brown.
Bott, Elizabeth
  1971   *Family and Social Network: Roles, Norms, and External Relationships in
         Ordinary Urban Families.* New York: Free Press (second edition; first
         edition, 1957).
Braithwaite, Richard Bevan
  1953   *Scientific Explanation: A Study of the Function of Theory, Probability and
         Law in Science.* New York: Harper and Row, 1960.
Bühler, Georg (translator)
  1886   *The Laws of Manu.* New York: Dover, 1969.
Burridge, Kenelm O.L.
  1957   "Disputing in Tangu." *American Anthropologist* 59 (October):763–780.
Cameron, Mary Owen
  1964   *The Booster and the Snitch: Department Store Shoplifting.* New York: Free
         Press.
Carlin, Jerome E., and Jan Howard
  1965   "Legal representation and class justice." *U.C.L.A. Law Review* 12
         (January):381–437.
Carlin, Jerome E., Jan Howard, and Sheldon L. Messinger
  1966   "Civil justice and the poor: issues for sociological research." *Law and
         Society Review* 1 (November):9–89.

Cartwright, B.C., and Richard D. Schwartz
1973 "The invocation of legal norms: an empirical investigation of Durkheim and Weber." *American Sociological Review* 38 (June):340–354.

Chambliss, William J.
1964 "A sociological analysis of the law of vagrancy." *Social Problems* 12 (Summer):67–77.
1967 "Types of deviance and the effectiveness of legal sanctions." *Wisconsin Law Review* 1967 (Summer):703–719.

Chambliss, William J., and Robert B. Seidman
1971 *Law, Order, and Power.* Reading: Addison-Wesley.

Chevigny, Paul
1969 *Police Power: Police Abuses in New York City.* New York: Vintage.

Cicourel, Aaron V.
1968 *The Social Organization of Juvenile Justice.* New York: John Wiley.

Clausen, John A., and Marion Radke Yarrow
1955 "Paths to the mental hospital." *Journal of Social Issues* 11 (Number 4):25–32.

Clébert, Jean-Paul
1961 *The Gypsies.* Baltimore: Penguin Books, 1967.

Clinard, Marshall B.
1946 "Criminological theories of violations of wartime regulations." *American Sociological Review* 11 (June):258–270.

Cloward, Richard A., and Lloyd E. Ohlin
1960 *Delinquency and Opportunity: A Theory of Delinquent Gangs.* New York: Free Press.

Cobb, R.C.
1970 *The Police and the People: French Popular Protest, 1789–1820.* London: Oxford University Press.

Cohen, Albert K.
1955 *Delinquent Boys: The Culture of the Gang.* New York: Free Press.

Cohn, Norman
1975 *Europe's Inner Demons: An Enquiry Inspired by the Great Witch-Hunt.* New York: Basic Books.

Colson, Elizabeth
1953 "Social control and vengeance in Plateau Tonga society." *Africa* 23 (July):199–212.

Conard, Alfred F., James N. Morgan, Robert W. Pratt, Jr., Charles E. Voltz, and Robert L. Bombaugh
1964 *Automobile Accident Costs and Payments: Studies in the Economics of Injury Reparation.* Ann Arbor: University of Michigan Press.

Coser, Lewis A.
1956 *The Functions of Social Conflict.* New York: Free Press.

Crane, Diana
1972 *Invisible Colleges: Diffusion of Knowledge in Scientific Communities.* Chicago: University of Chicago Press.

Currie, Elliott P.
1968 "Crimes without criminals: witchcraft and its control in Renaissance Europe." *Law and Society Review* 3 (August):7–32.

Curtis, Richard F.
    1963 "Differential association and the stratification of the urban community."
        Social Forces 42 (October):68–77.

Dahrendorf, Ralf
    1959 *Class and Class Conflict in Industrial Society.* Stanford: Stanford University
        Press (revised edition; first edition, 1957).
    1968a "On the origin of inequality among men." Pages 151–178 in *Essays in the*
        Theory of Society. Stanford: Stanford University Press (revised version;
        first version, 1961).
    1968b "In praise of Thrasymachus." Pages 129–150 in *Essays in the Theory of*
        Society. Stanford: Stanford University Press.

Davis, Kenneth Culp
    1969 *Discretionary Justice: A Preliminary Inquiry.* Baton Rouge: Louisiana State
        University Press.

Davis, Kingsley, and Wilbert E. Moore
    1945 "Some principles of stratification." *American Sociological Review* 10
        (April):242–249.

Demos, John
    1970a *A Little Commonwealth: Family Life in Plymouth Colony.* New York: Oxford
        University Press.
    1970b "Underlying themes in the witchcraft of seventeenth-century New Eng-
        land." *American Historical Review* 75 (June):1311–1326.

Deutsch, Karl
    1968 "The probability of international law." Pages 80–114 in *The Relevance of*
        International Law, edited by K. Deutsch and Stanley Hoffmann. Garden
        City: Anchor Books, 1971.

Dicey, A.V.
    1905 *Lectures on the Relation between Law and Public Opinion in England during*
        the Nineteenth Century. London: Macmillan.

Dinitz, Simon, Mark Lefton, Shirley Angrist, and Benjamin Pasamanick
    1961 "Psychiatric and social attributes as predictors of case outcome in mental
        hospitalization." *Social Problems* 8 (Spring):322–328.

Dollard, John, Neal E. Miller, Leonard W. Doob, O.H. Mowrer, and Robert R. Sears
(in collaboration with Clellan S. Ford, Carl Iver Hovland, and Richard T. Sollenberger)
    1939 *Frustration and Aggression.* New Haven: Yale University Press.

Douglas, Mary
    1973 *Natural Symbols: Explorations in Cosmology.* New York: Vintage Books
        (revised edition; first edition, 1970).

Downes, T.W.
    1929 "Maori etiquette." *Journal of the Polynesian Society* 38 (June):148–168.

Doyle, Bertram Wilbur
    1937 *The Etiquette of Race Relations in the South: A Study in Social Control.*
        Chicago: University of Chicago Press.

Dresch, Stephen P.
    1973 "Legal rights and the rites of passage: experience, education and the
        obsolescence of adolescence." Working Paper W3-39, Center for the
        Study of the City and Its Environment, Yale University.

Drucker, Philip
　　1939　"Rank, wealth, and kinship in Northwest Coast society." *American Anthropologist* 41 (January–March):55–65.
Durkheim, Emile
　　1893　*The Division of Labor in Society.* New York: Free Press, 1964.
　　1897　*Suicide: A Study in Sociology.* New York: Free Press, 1951.
　　1899–　"Two laws of penal evolution." *University of Cincinnati Law Review*
　　1900　38 (Winter, 1969):32–60.
　　1950　*Professional Ethics and Civic Morals.* New York: Free Press, 1958.
Durkheim, Emile, and Marcel Mauss
　　1903　*Primitive Classification.* Chicago: University of Chicago Press, 1963.
Engels, Friedrich
　　1878　*Herr Eugen Dühring's Revolution in Science (Anti-Dühring).* New York: International Publishers, 1939.
　　1884　*The Origin of the Family, Private Property and the State: In the Light of the Researches of Lewis H. Morgan.* New York: International Publishers, 1942.
　　1888　Ludwig Feuerbach and the End of Classical German Philosophy. Pages 195–242 in *Basic Writings on Politics and Philosophy,* edited by Lewis S. Feuer. Garden City: Anchor Books, 1959.
　　1890　"Letter to Conrad Schmidt." Pages 400–407 in *Basic Writings on Politics and Philosophy,* edited by Lewis S. Feuer. Garden City: Anchor Books, 1959.
Ennis, Philip H.
　　1967　*Criminal Victimization in the United States: A Report of a National Survey.* A Report to the President's Commission on Law Enforcement and Administration of Justice. Washington, D.C.: U.S. Government Printing Office.
Epstein, A.L.
　　1951　"Some aspects of the conflict of law and urban courts in Northern Rhodesia." *Rhodes–Livingstone Journal* 12 (December):28–40.
　　1953　"The role of African courts in urban communities of the Northern Rhodesia Copperbelt." *Rhodes–Livingstone Journal* 13 (July):1–17.
　　1954　"Divorce law and the stability of marriage among the Lunda of Kazembe." *Rhodes–Livingstone Journal* 14 (December):1–19.
　　1958　*Politics in an Urban African Community.* Manchester: Manchester University Press.
Erikson, Kai T.
　　1962　"Notes on the sociology of deviance." *Social Problems* 9 (Spring):307–314.
　　1966　*Wayward Puritans: A Study in the Sociology of Deviance.* New York: John Wiley.
Etzioni, Amitai
　　1961　*A Comparative Analysis of Complex Organizations.* New York: Free Press.
　　1965　"Organizational control structure." Pages 650–677 in *Handbook of Organizations,* edited by James G. March. Chicago: Rand McNally.
Evan, William M.
　　1959　"Power, bargaining, and law: a preliminary analysis of labor arbitration cases." *Social Problems* 7 (Summer):4–15.

Evans-Pritchard, E.E.
    1937   *Witchcraft, Oracles and Magic among the Azande.* London: Oxford University Press.
    1940a   *The Nuer: A Description of the Modes of Livelihood and Political Institutions of a Nilotic People.* London: Oxford University Press.
    1940b   "The Nuer of the southern Sudan." Pages 272–296 in *African Political Systems,* edited by M. Fortes and E.E. Evans-Pritchard. London: Oxford University Press.

Fallers, Lloyd A.
    1956   "Changing customary law in Busoga District of Uganda." *Journal of African Administration* 8 (July):139–144.
    1969   *Law without Precedent: Legal Ideas in Action in the Courts of Colonial Busoga.* Chicago: University of Chicago Press.
    1973   *Inequality: Social Stratification Reconsidered.* Chicago: University of Chicago Press.

Feldman, Harvey W.
    1968   "Ideological supports to becoming and remaining a heroin addict." *Journal of Health and Social Behavior* 9 (June):131–139.

Field, M.J.
    1960   *Search for Security: An Ethno-Psychiatric Study of Rural Ghana.* New York: W. W. Norton, 1970.

Firth, Raymond
    1951   *Elements of Social Organization.* New York: Philosophical Library.

Fortes, M.
    1940   "The political system of the Tallensi of the northern territories of the Gold Coast." Pages 239–271 in *African Political Systems,* edited by M. Fortes and E.E. Evans-Pritchard. London: Oxford University Press.

Fortes, M., and E.E. Evans-Pritchard
    1940   "Introduction." Pages 1–23 in *African Political Systems,* edited by M. Fortes and E.E. Evans-Pritchard. London: Oxford University Press.

Fried, Morton H.
    1960   "On the evolution of social stratification and the state." Pages 713–731 in *Culture in History: Essays in Honor of Paul Radin,* edited by Stanley Diamond. New York: Columbia University Press.
    1967   *The Evolution of Political Society: An Essay in Political Anthropology.* New York: Random House.

Fritz, Kathlyn
    1971   "A cross-cultural study of witchcraft and legal control." *Yale Sociology Journal* 1 (Spring):1–22.

Fuller, Lon L.
    1969   "Two principles of human association." Pages 3–23 in *Voluntary Associations* (*Nomos,* Volume 11), edited by J. Rolland Pennock and John W. Chapman. New York: Atherton Press.

Furnivall, J.S.
    1948   *Colonial Policy and Practice: A Comparative Study of Burma and Netherlands India.* Cambridge: Cambridge University Press.

Fustel de Coulanges, Numa Denis
  1864 *The Ancient City: A Study on the Religion, Laws, and Institutions of Greece and Rome.* Garden City: Anchor Books, 1956.
Galanter, Marc
  1974 "Why the 'haves' come out ahead: speculations on the limits of legal change." *Law and Society Review* 9 (Fall):95–160.
  1975 "Afterword: explaining litigation." *Law and Society Review* 9 (Winter):346–368.
Gallin, Bernard
  1966 "Conflict resolution in changing Chinese society: a Taiwanese study." Pages 265–274 in *Political Anthropology*, edited by Marc J. Swartz, Victor W. Turner, and Arthur Tuden. Chicago: Aldine.
Garfinkel, Harold
  1949 "Research note on inter- and intra-racial homicides." *Social Forces* 27 (May):369–381.
  1956 "Conditions of successful degradation ceremonies." *American Journal of Sociology* 61 (March):420–424.
Garnsey, Peter
  1968 "Legal privilege in the Roman Empire." *Past and Present: A Journal of Historical Studies* 41 (December):3–24.
Geertz, Clifford
  1963 *Agricultural Involution: The Process of Ecological Change in Indonesia.* Berkeley: University of California Press.
Ghai, Y.P.
  1969 "Customary contracts and transactions in Kenya." Pages 333–344 in *Ideas and Procedures in African Customary Law*, edited by Max Gluckman. London: Oxford University Press.
Gibbs, James L., Jr.
  1962 "Poro values and courtroom procedures in a Kpelle courtroom." *Southwestern Journal of Anthropology* 18 (Winter):341–350.
  1963 "The Kpelle moot: a therapeutic model for the informal settlement of disputes." *Africa* 33 (January):1–10.
Gillin, John
  1934 "Crime and punishment among the Barama River Carib of British Guiana." *American Anthropologist* 36 (July–August):331–344.
Glenn, Norval D., and Jon P. Alston
  1968 "Cultural distances among occupational categories." *American Sociological Review* 33 (June):365–382.
Gluckman, Max
  1962 "African jurisprudence." *The Advancement of Science* 75 (January):439–454.
  1965 *The Ideas in Barotse Jurisprudence.* New Haven: Yale University Press.
  1967 *The Judicial Process among the Barotse of Northern Rhodesia.* Manchester: Manchester University Press (second edition; first edition, 1955).
Goffman, Erving
  1956 "The nature of deference and demeanor." *American Anthropologist* 58 (June):473–502.

1959a "The moral career of the mental patient." Pages 125–169 in *Asylums: Essays on the Social Situation of Mental Patients and Other Inmates*. Garden City: Anchor Books, 1961.

1959b *The Presentation of Self in Everyday Life*. Garden City: Anchor Books.

1961a "On the characteristics of total institutions." Pages 1–124 in *Asylums: Essays on the Social Situation of Mental Patients and Other Inmates*. Garden City: Anchor Books (enlarged version; first version, 1957).

1961b "Role distance." Pages 83–152 in *Encounters: Two Studies in the Sociology of Interaction*. Indianapolis: Bobbs-Merrill.

1963 *Behavior in Public Places: Notes on the Social Organization of Gatherings*. New York: Free Press.

1971 *Relations in Public: Microstudies of the Public Order*. New York: Basic Books.

Goldenweiser, Alexander A.

1936 "Loose ends of theory on the individual, pattern, and involution in primitive society." Pages 99–104 in *Essays in Anthropology Presented to A.L. Kroeber in Celebration of His Sixtieth Birthday, June 11, 1936*, edited by Robert H. Lowie. Berkeley: University of California Press.

Goldman, Irving

1955 "Status rivalry and cultural evolution in Polynesia." *American Anthropologist* 57 (August):680–697.

Gough, E. Kathleen

1960 "Caste in a Tanjore village." Pages 11–60 in *Aspects of Caste in South India, Ceylon and North-West Pakistan*, edited by E.R. Leach. Cambridge: Cambridge University Press.

Gouldner, Alvin W.

1954 *Patterns of Industrial Bureaucracy*. Glencoe: Free Press.

Gove, Walter R.

1970 "Societal reaction as an explanation of mental illness: an evaluation." *American Sociological Review* 35 (October):873–884.

Grace, Roger

1970 "Justice, Chinese style." *Case and Comment* 75 (January–February):50–51.

Granovetter, Mark S.

1973 "The strength of weak ties." *American Journal of Sociology* 78 (May):1360–1380.

Green, Edward

1964 "Inter- and intra-racial crime relative to sentencing." *Journal of Criminal Law, Criminology and Police Science* 55 (September):348–358.

Greuel, Peter J.

1971 "The leopard-skin chief: an examination of political power among the Nuer." *American Anthropologist* 73 (October):1115–1120.

Gulliver, Philip H.

1963 *Social Control in an African Society: A Study of the Arusha, Agricultural Masai of Northern Tanganyika*. Boston: Boston University Press.

1969 "Dispute settlement without courts: the Ndendeuli of southern Tanzania." Pages 24–68 in *Law in Culture and Society*, edited by Laura Nader. Chicago: Aldine.

Gurr, Ted Robert
1970 *Why Men Rebel.* Princeton: Princeton University Press.
Gusfield, Joseph
1963 *Symbolic Crusade: Status Politics and the American Temperance Movement.* Urbana: University of Illinois Press.
Gusinde, Martin
1937 *Die Feuerland Indianer.* Mödling bei Wien: Verlag Anthropos. Band 2: Die Yamana; von Leben und Denken der Wassernomaden am Kap Hoorn.
Haar, B. ter
1939 *Adat Law in Indonesia.* New York: Institute of Pacific Relations, 1948.
Hagan, John
1974 "Extra-legal attributes and criminal sentencing: an assessment of a sociological viewpoint." *Law and Society Review* 8 (Spring):357–383.
Hagan, William T.
1966 *Indian Police and Judges: Experiments in Acculturation and Control.* New Haven: Yale University Press.
Hall, Edwin L., and Albert A. Simkus
1975 "Inequality in the types of sentences received by native Americans and whites." *Criminology* 13 (August):199–222.
Hall, Jerome
1952 *Theft, Law, and Society.* Indianapolis: Bobbs-Merrill (second edition; first edition, 1935).
Harper, Robert Francis (translator)
1904 *The Code of Hammurabi, King of Babylon: About 2250 B.C.* Chicago: University of Chicago Press.
Haskins, George Lee
1960 *Law and Authority in Early Massachusetts: A Study in Tradition and Design.* Hamden: Archon Books, 1968.
Hasluck, Margaret
1954 *The Unwritten Law in Albania.* Cambridge: Cambridge University Press.
Hast, Adele
1969 "The legal status of the Negro in Virginia, 1705–1765." *Journal of Negro History* 54 (July):217–239.
Hegel, Georg Wilhelm Friedrich
1821 *Hegel's Philosophy of Right.* London: Oxford University Press, 1952.
Hempel, Carl G.
1965 "Aspects of scientific explanation." Pages 331–496 in *Aspects of Scientific Explanation and Other Essays in the Philosophy of Science.* New York: Free Press.
Henry, Andrew F., and James F. Short, Jr.
1954 *Suicide and Homicide: Some Economic, Sociological and Psychological Aspects of Aggression.* Glencoe: Free Press.
Hippler, Arthur E., and Stephen Conn
1973 "Northern Eskimo law ways and their relationship to contemporary problems of 'bush justice': some preliminary observations on structure and function." ISEGR Occasional Papers, Number 10. Fairbanks: Uni-

versity of Alaska, Institute of Social, Economic, and Government Research.

Hirschi, Travis
1969 *Causes of Delinquency*. Berkeley: University of California Press.

Hobhouse, L.T.
1951 *Morals in Evolution: A Study in Comparative Ethics*. London: Chapman and Hall.

Hoebel, E. Adamson
1940 *The Political Organization and Law-Ways of the Comanche Indians*. Memoirs of the American Anthropological Association, Number 54. Menasha: American Anthropological Association.
1954 *The Law of Primitive Man: A Study in Comparative Legal Dynamics*. Cambridge: Harvard University Press.
1965 "Fundamental cultural postulates and judicial lawmaking in Pakistan." Pages 43–56 in *The Ethnography of Law*, edited by Laura Nader. Published as supplement to *American Anthropologist*, Volume 67, December.
1969 "Keresan Pueblo law." Pages 92–116 in *Law in Culture and Society*, edited by Laura Nader. Chicago: Aldine.
1970 "How advanced is our legal system? a look by a primitive lawyer." Unpublished paper presented to the UPI Editors' and Publishers' Conference, Colonial Williamsburg, October 13.

Hogbin, H. Ian
1934 *Law and Order in Polynesia: A Study of Primitive Legal Institutions*. New York: Harcourt.

Hollander, E.P.
1958 "Conformity, status, and idiosyncrasy credit." *Psychological Review* 65 (March):117–127.
1960 "Competence and conformity in the acceptance of influence." *Journal of Abnormal and Social Psychology* 61 (November):365–369.

Hollingshead, August B.
1941 "The concept of social control." *American Sociological Review* 6 (April):217–224.

Hollingshead, August B., and Fredrick C. Redlich
1958 *Social Class and Mental Illness: A Community Study*. New York: John Wiley.

Homans, George Caspar
1964 "Contemporary theory in sociology." Pages 951–977 in *Handbook of Modern Sociology*, edited by Robert E.L. Faris. Chicago: Rand McNally.
1967 *The Nature of Social Science*. New York: Harcourt.

Horwitz, Allan Victor
1975 Social Networks and Pathways into Psychiatric Treatment. Unpublished doctoral dissertation, Department of Sociology, Yale University.

Howell, P.P.
1954 *A Manual of Nuer Law: Being an Account of Customary Law, Its Evolution and Development in the Courts Established by the Sudan Government*. London: Oxford University Press.

Hunt, Eva, and Robert Hunt
    1969   "The role of courts in rural Mexico." Pages 109–139 in *Peasants in the Modern World*, edited by Philip K. Bock. University Park: University of New Mexico Press.
Hunting, Roger Bryant, and Gloria S. Neuwirth
    1962   *Who Sues in New York City: A Study of Automobile Accident Claims.* New York: Columbia University Press.
Inglis, Amirah
    1974   *"Not a White Woman Safe": Sexual Anxiety and Politics in Port Moresby, 1920–1934.* Canberra: Australian National University Press.
Irwin, John
    1970   *The Felon.* Englewood Cliffs: Prentice-Hall.
Jeffreys, M.D.W.
    1952   "Samsonic suicide or suicide of revenge among Africans." *African Studies* 11 (September):118–122.
Johnson, G.B.
    1941   "The Negro and crime." *The Annals of the American Academy of Political and Social Science* 271 (September):93–104.
Johnson, Gregory Alan
    1973   *Local Exchange and Early State Development in Southwestern Iran.* Ann Arbor: University of Michigan Museum of Anthropology. Anthropological Papers, Number 51.
Jouvenel, Bertrand de
    1961   "The Republic of Science." Pages 131–141 in *The Logic of Personal Knowledge: Essays Presented to Michael Polanyi on His Seventieth Birthday, 11th March 1961.* Glencoe: Free Press.
Karst, Kenneth L., Murray L. Schwartz, and Audrey J. Schwartz
    1973   *The Evolution of Law in the Barrios of Caracas.* Los Angeles: University of California, Latin American Center.
Karsten, Rafael
    1923   *Blood Revenge, War, and Victory Feasts among the Jibaro Indians of Eastern Equador.* Bureau of American Ethnology, Bulletin 79. Washington, D.C.: Government Printing Office.
Kawashima, Takeyoshi
    1963   "Dispute resolution in contemporary Japan." Pages 41–72 in *Law in Japan: The Legal Order in a Changing Society*, edited by Arthur T. von Mehren. Cambridge: Harvard University Press.
Kelley, Jonathan
    1976   The Birth of Privilege: Resources, Modernization and Mobility.   Unpublished manuscript, Department of Sociology, Yale University.
Kelsen, Hans
    1968   "The essence of international law." Pages 115–123 in *The Relevance of International Law*, edited by Karl Deutsch and Stanley Hoffmann. Garden City: Anchor Books, 1971.
Kessler, Friedrich
    1943   "Contracts of adhesion—some thoughts about freedom of contract." *Columbia Law Review* 43 (July):629–642.
    1957   "Automobile dealer franchises: vertical integration by contract." *Yale Law Journal* 66 (July):217–239.

Kitsuse, John I., and Aaron V. Cicourel
   1963   "A note on the uses of official statistics." *Social Problems* 11 (Fall):131–
          139.
Kluckhohn, Clyde
   1944   *Navajo Witchcraft.* Boston: Beacon Press, 1967.
Krause, Aurel
   1885   *The Tlingit Indians: Results of a Trip to the Northwest Coast of America and
          the Bering Straits.* Seattle: University of Washington Press, 1956.
Ladinsky, Jack
   1963   "Careers of lawyers, law practice, and legal institutions." *American
          Sociological Review* 28 (February):47–54.
La Fave, Wayne R.
   1965   *Arrest: The Decision to Take a Suspect into Custody.* Boston: Little, Brown.
Lantis, Margaret
   1946   "The social culture of the Nunivak Eskimo." *Transactions of the American
          Philosophical Society* 35(Part 3):153–323.
Laumann, Edward O.
   1966   *Prestige and Association in an Urban Community: An Analysis of an Urban
          Stratification System.* Indianapolis: Bobbs-Merrill.
Lemert, Edwin M.
   1948   "Some aspects of a general theory of sociopathic behavior." *Proceedings
          of the Meetings of the Pacific Sociological Society* 16: 23–29.
   1951   *Social Pathology.* New York: McGraw-Hill.
   1962   "Paranoia and the dynamics of exclusion." *Sociometry* 25 (March): 2–20.
   1964   "Social structure, social control, and deviation." Pages 57–97 in *Anomie
          and Deviant Behavior: A Discussion and Critique,* edited by Marshall B.
          Clinard. New York: Free Press.
   1967   "The concept of secondary deviation." Pages 40–64 in *Human Deviance,
          Social Problems, and Social Control.* Englewood Cliffs: Prentice-Hall.
Leslie, Robert D.
   1969   "Lesotho, Botswana, and Swaziland." Pages 167–189 in *African Penal
          Systems,* edited by Alan Milner. New York: Frederick A. Praeger.
Lévi-Strauss, Claude
   1955   *Tristes Tropiques: An Anthropological Study of Primitive Societies in Brazil.*
          New York: Atheneum, 1963.
Lévy-Bruhl, Henri
   1951   "The sources of law: outlines of a theory." *University of Cincinnati Law
          Review* 38 (Number 4, 1969):663–689.
Linton, Ralph
   1936   *The Study of Man: An Introduction.* New York: Appleton-Century-Crofts.
Lintott, A. W.
   1968   *Violence in Republican Rome.* London: Oxford University Press.
Lipset, Seymour Martin
   1960   *Political Man: The Social Bases of Politics.* Garden City: Anchor Books.
Llewellyn, Karl N., and E. Adamson Hoebel
   1941   *The Cheyenne Way: Conflict and Case Law in Primitive Jurisprudence.* Nor-
          man: University of Oklahoma Press.
Lofland, John (with the assistance of Lyn H. Lofland)
   1969   *Deviance and Identity.* Englewood Cliffs: Prentice-Hall.

Lofland, John, and Rodney Stark
    1965 "Becoming a world-saver: a theory of conversion to a deviant perspective." *American Sociological Review* 30 (December):862–875.
Lofland, Lyn H.
    1973 *A World of Strangers: Order and Action in Urban Public Space.* New York: Basic Books.
Lowenstein, Steven
    1969 "Ethiopia." Pages 35–57 in *African Penal Systems,* edited by Alan Milner. New York: Frederick A. Praeger.
Lowie, Robert H.
    1927 *The Origin of the State.* New York: Harcourt.
    1948 "Some aspects of political organization among the American aborigines." *Journal of the Royal Anthropological Institute of Great Britain and Ireland* 78: 11–24.
Luttwak, Edward
    1969 *Coup d'État: A Practical Handbook.* New York: Alfred A. Knopf.
Lyman, Stanford M., and Marvin B. Scott
    1967 "Territoriality: a neglected sociological dimension." *Social Problems* 15 (Fall):236–249.
Macaulay, Stewart
    1963 "Non-contractual relations in business: a preliminary study." *American Sociological Review* 28 (February): 55–67.
    1966 *Law and the Balance of Power: The Automobile Manufacturers and Their Dealers.* New York: Russell Sage Foundation.
Macfarlane, Alan
    1970 *Witchcraft in Tudor and Stuart England: A Regional and Comparative Study.* New York: Harper and Row.
MacLeod, William Christie
    1937 "Police and punishment among native Americans of the Plains." *Journal of the American Institute of Criminal Law and Criminology* 28 (July–August):181–201.
Maine, Henry Sumner
    1861 *Ancient Law: Its Connection with the Early History of Society and Its Relation to Modern Ideas.* Boston: Beacon Press, 1963.
Malinowski, Bronislaw
    1926 *Crime and Custom in Savage Society.* Paterson: Littlefield, Adams, 1962.
Mannheim, Karl
    1927 "Conservative thought." Pages 74–164 in *Essays on Sociology and Social Psychology,* edited by Paul Kecskemeti. New York: Oxford University Press, 1953.
Marcuse, Herbert
    1955 *Eros and Civilization: A Philosophical Inquiry into Freud.* Boston: Beacon Press.
Marwick, Max
    1964 "Witchcraft as a social strain-gauge." *Australian Journal of Science* 26 (March):263–268.
    1965 "Some problems in the sociology of sorcery and witchcraft." Pages 171–

191 in *African Systems of Thought: Studies Presented and Discussed at the Third International African Seminar in Salisbury, December 1961,* edited by M. Fortes and G. Dieterlen. London: Oxford University Press.

1970 "The decline of witch-beliefs in differentiated societies." Pages 379–382 in *Witchcraft and Sorcery: Selected Readings,* edited by M. Marwick. Baltimore: Penguin Books.

Marx, Karl
1890 *Capital: A Critique of Political Economy.* New York: International Publishers, 1967 (fourth edition; first edition, 1867). Volume 1: The Process of Capitalist Production.

Marx, Karl, and Friedrich Engels
1888 Manifesto of the Communist Party. Pages 1–41 in *Basic Writings on Politics and Philosophy,* edited by Lewis S. Feuer. Garden City: Anchor Books, 1959 (annotated English edition; first edition, 1848).

Massell, Gregory
1968 "Law as an instrument of revolutionary change in a traditional milieu: the case of Soviet Central Asia." *Law and Society Review* 2 (February):179–211.

Matza, David
1964 *Delinquency and Drift.* New York: John Wiley.
1969 *Becoming Deviant.* Englewood Cliffs: Prentice-Hall.

Mauss, M. (with the collaboration of M.H. Beuchat)
1905– "Essai sur les variations saisonnières des sociétés Eskimos: étude de
1906 morphologie sociale." *L'Année sociologique* 9:39–132.

Mayhew, Leon H.
1968 *Law and Equal Opportunity: A Study of the Massachusetts Commission Against Discrimination.* Cambridge: Harvard University Press.
1975 "Institutions of representation: civil justice and the public." *Law and Society Review* 9 (Spring): 401–429.

Mayhew, Leon H., and Albert J. Reiss, Jr.
1969 "The social organization of legal contacts." *American Sociological Review* 34 (June):309–318.

McIntyre, Jennie
1967 "Public attitudes toward crime and law enforcement." *The Annals of the American Academy of Political and Social Science* 374 (November):34–46.

Meggitt, M.J.
1962 *Desert People: A Study of the Walbiri Aborigines of Central Australia.* Sydney: Angus and Robertson.

Merton, Robert K.
1938a "Social structure and anomie." *American Sociological Review* 3 (October):672–682.
1938b *Science, Technology and Society in Seventeenth-Century England.* New York: Harper and Row, 1970.
1942 "Science and technology in a democratic order." Pages 267–278 in *The Sociology of Science: Theoretical and Empirical Investigations.* Chicago: University of Chicago Press, 1973.
1957 "Priorities in scientific discovery: a chapter in the sociology of science."

Pages 286–324 in *The Sociology of Science: Theoretical and Empirical Investigations*. Chicago: University of Chicago Press, 1973.

1968 "The Matthew effect in science." *Science* 159 (January 5):55–63.

Michels, Robert
1911 *Political Parties: A Sociological Study of the Oligarchical Tendencies of Modern Democracy*. New York: Collier Books, 1962.

Middleton, John
1956 "The role of chiefs and headmen among the Lugbara of West Nile District, Uganda." *Journal of African Administration* 8 (January):32–38.

1958 "The political system of the Lugbara of the Nile–Congo divide." Pages 203–229 in *Tribes without Rulers: Studies in African Segmentary Systems*, edited by J. Middleton and David Tait. New York: Humanities Press, 1970.

1965 *The Lugbara of Uganda*. New York: Holt, Rinehart, and Winston.

Midelfort, H.C. Erik
1972 *Witch Hunting in Southwestern Germany, 1562–1684: The Social and Intellectual Foundations*. Stanford: Stanford University Press.

Mileski, Maureen
1971 "Courtroom encounters: an observation study of a lower criminal court." *Law and Society Review* 5 (May):473–538.

Miller, Daniel R., and Guy E. Swanson
1958 *The Changing American Parent: A Study in the Detroit Area*. New York: John Wiley.

Miller, Walter B.
1958 "Lower class culture as a generating milieu of gang delinquency." *Journal of Social Issues* 14 (Number 3):5–19.

Mitchell, J. Clyde
1965 "The meaning in misfortune for urban Africans." Pages 192–203 in *African Systems of Thought: Studies Presented and Discussed at the Third International African Seminar in Salisbury, December 1960*, edited by M. Fortes and G. Dieterlen. London: Oxford University Press.

1969 "The concept and use of social networks." Pages 1–50 in *Social Networks in Urban Situations: Analyses of Personal Relationships in Central African Towns*, edited by J.C. Mitchell. Manchester: Manchester University Press.

Montesquieu, Baron de
1748 *The Spirit of the Laws*. New York: Hafner, 1949. Volume 2.

Moore, Barrington, Jr.
1942 "The relation between social stratification and social control." *Sociometry* 5 (August):230–250.

1966 *Social Origins of Dictatorship and Democracy: Lord and Peasant in the Making of the Modern World*. Boston: Beacon Press.

Moore, Sally Falk
1958 *Power and Property in Inca Peru*. New York: Columbia University Press.

Morgan, Lewis Henry
1877 *Ancient Society*. Cambridge: Harvard University Press, 1964.

Myers, Jerome K., and Leslie Schaffer
1954 "Social stratification and psychiatric practice: a study of an outpatient clinic." *American Sociological Review* 19 (June):307–310.

Myrdal, Gunnar (with the assistance of Richard Sterner and Arnold Rose)
    1944   *An American Dilemma: The Negro Problem and Modern Democracy.* New York: Harper and Brothers.

Nadel, S.F.
    1942   *A Black Byzantium: The Kingdom of Nupe in Nigeria.* London: Oxford University Press.

Nader, Laura
    1965   "Choices in legal procedure: Shia Moslem and Mexican Zapotec." *American Anthropologist* 67 (April):394–399.
    1969   "Styles of court procedure: to make the balance." Pages 69–91 in *Law in Culture and Society,* edited by L. Nader. Chicago: Aldine.

Nader, Laura, and Duane Metzger
    1963   "Conflict resolution in two Mexican communities." *American Anthropologist* 65 (June):584–592.

Nimuendajú, Curt
    1939   *The Apinayé.* Washington, D.C.: The Catholic University of America Press.

Nisbet, Robert
    1964   "Kinship and political power in First Century Rome." Pages 257–271 in *Sociology and History,* edited by Werner J. Cahnman and Alvin Boskoff. New York: Free Press.

Nohl, Johannes
    1926   *The Black Death: A Chronicle of the Plague Compiled from Contemporary Sources.* London: Unwin Books, 1961.

Noon, John A.
    1949   *Law and Government of the Grand River Iroquois.* New York: Viking Fund Publications in Anthropology, Number 12.

Nye, F. Ivan, James F. Short, Jr., and Virgil J. Olson
    1958   "Socioeconomic status and delinquent behavior." *American Journal of Sociology* 63 (January):381–389.

Oberschall, Anthony
    1973   *Social Conflict and Social Movements.* Englewood Cliffs: Prentice-Hall.

Olson, Mancur, Jr.
    1965   *The Logic of Collective Action: Public Goods and the Theory of Groups.* New York: Schocken Books, 1968.

Orenstein, Henry
    1968   "Toward a grammar of defilement in Hindu sacred law." Pages 115–131 in *Structure and Change in Indian Society,* edited by Milton Singer and Bernard S. Cohn. New York: Wenner-Gren Foundation.

Paglin, Morton
    1975   "The measurement and trend of inequality: a basic revision." *American Economic Review* 65 (September):598–609.

Park, Robert E.
    1924   "The concept of social distance as applied to the study of racial attitudes and racial relations." *Journal of Applied Sociology* 8 (July–August):339–344.

Parsons, Talcott
    1940   "An analytical approach to the theory of social stratification." Pages

69–88 in *Essays in Sociological Theory.* New York: Free Press, 1954 (revised edition; first edition, 1949).

1951 *The Social System.* New York: Free Press.

1962 "The law and social control." Pages 56–72 in *Law and Sociology: Exploratory Essays,* edited by William M. Evan. New York: Free Press.

1966 *Societies: Evolutionary and Comparative Perspectives.* Englewood Cliffs: Prentice-Hall.

Parsons, Talcott, and Edward A. Shils (with the assistance of James Olds)

1951 "Values, motives, and systems of action." Pages 47–243 in *Toward a General Theory of Action,* edited by T. Parsons and E.A. Shils. New York: Harper and Row.

Parsons, Talcott, Edward A. Shils, Gordon W. Allport, Clyde Kluckhohn, Henry A. Murray, Robert R. Sears, Richard C. Sheldon, Samuel A. Stouffer, and Edward C. Tolman

1951 "Some fundamental categories of the theory of action: a general statement." Pages 3–29 in *Toward a General Theory of Action,* edited by T. Parsons and E.A. Shils. New York: Harper and Row.

Peattie, Lisa Redfield

1968 *The View from the Barrio.* Ann Arbor: University of Michigan Press.

Peters, E. Lloyd

1967 "Some structural aspects of the feud among the camel-herding Bedouin of Cyrenaica." *Africa* 37 (July):261–282.

1972 "Aspects of the control of moral ambiguities: a comparative analysis of two culturally disparate modes of social control." Pages 109–162 in *The Allocation of Responsibility,* edited by Max Gluckman. Manchester: Manchester University Press.

Piaget, Jean (with the assistance of seven collaborators)

1932 *The Moral Judgment of the Child.* New York: Free Press, 1965.

Pike, Luke Owen

1873 *A History of Crime in England: Illustrating the Changes of the Laws in the Progress of Civilization.* London: Smith, Elder. Volume 1: From the Roman Invasion to the Accession of Henry VII.

1876 *A History of Crime in England: Illustrating the Changes of the Laws in the Progress of Civilization.* London: Smith, Elder. Volume 2: From the Accession of Henry VII to the Present Time.

Polanyi, Karl (in collaboration with Abraham Rotstein)

1966 *Dahomey and the Slave Trade: An Analysis of an Archaic Economy.* Seattle: University of Washington Press.

Polanyi, Michael

1946 *Science, Faith and Society.* London: Oxford University Press.

Pollock, Frederick, and Frederic William Maitland

1898 *The History of English Law: Before the Time of Edward I.* Cambridge: Cambridge University Press, 1968 (second edition; first edition, 1895).

Pospisil, Leopold

1958 *Kapauku Papuans and Their Law.* New Haven: Yale University Publications in Anthropology, Number 54.

1971 *Anthropology of Law: A Comparative Theory.* New York: Harper and Row.

Pound, Roscoe
    1939   *The History and System of the Common Law*. New York: P. F. Collier.
    1942   *Social Control through Law*. New Haven: Yale University Press.

Powers, Edwin
    1966   *Crime and Punishment in Early Massachusetts, 1626–1692: A Documentary History*. Boston: Beacon Press.

Prucha, Francis Paul
    1962   *American Indian Policy in the Formative Years: The Indian Trade and Intercourse Acts, 1790–1834*. Lincoln: University of Nebraska Press.

Quinney, Richard
    1974   *Critique of Legal Order: Crime Control in Capitalist Society*. Boston: Little, Brown.

Radcliffe-Brown, A.R.
    1933   "Primitive law." Pages 213–219 in *Structure and Function in Primitive Society: Essays and Addresses*. New York: Free Press, 1965.
    1935   "On the concept of function in social science." Pages 178–187 in *Structure and Function in Primitive Society: Essays and Addresses*. New York: Free Press, 1965.
    1940   "On joking relationships." Pages 90–104 in *Structure and Function in Primitive Society: Essays and Addresses*. New York: Free Press, 1965.

Redfield, Robert
    1947   "The folk society." *American Journal of Sociology* 52 (January):293–308.
    1955   The Little Community. Pages 1–182 in *The Little Community and Peasant Society and Culture*. Chicago: University of Chicago Press, 1960.
    1964   "Primitive law." *University of Cincinnati Law Review* 33 (Winter):1–22.

Rees, Alwyn D.
    1950   *Life in a Welsh Countryside: A Social Study of Llanfihangel yng Ngwynfa*. Cardiff: University of Wales Press.

Reiss, Albert J., Jr.
    1951   "Delinquency as the failure of personal and social controls." *American Sociological Review* 16 (April):196–207.
    1966   "The study of deviant behavior: where the action is." *The Ohio Valley Sociologist* 32 (Autumn):1–12.
    1967   "Measurement of the nature and amount of crime." Pages 1–183 in *Studies in Crime and Law Enforcement in Major Metropolitan Areas*. A Report to the President's Commission on Law Enforcement and Administration of Justice. Washington, D.C.: U.S. Government Printing Office. Volume 1.

Reiss, Albert J., Jr., and Albert Lewis Rhodes
    1961   "The distribution of juvenile delinquency in the social class structure." *American Sociological Review* 26 (October):720–732.

Robin, Gerald D.
    1967   "The corporate and judicial disposition of employee thieves." *Wisconsin Law Review* 1967 (Summer):685–702.

Ross, Edward Alsworth
    1901   *Social Control: A Survey of the Foundations of Order*. New York: Macmillan.

Rousseau, Jean-Jacques
    1762a *Emilius and Sophia: Or, A New System of Education.* London: T. Becket and
        P.A. de Hondt, 1763. Volume 2.
    1762b *The Social Contract: Or, Principles of Political Right.* Middlesex: Penguin
        Books, 1968.
Rubin, Sol
    1966 "Disparity and equality of sentences—a constitutional challenge." *Fed-
        eral Rules Decisions* 40 (February):55–78.
Rudel, Thomas K.
    1973 "Social morphology and the evolution of property law." Unpublished
        paper, Department of Sociology, Yale University.
Rusche, Georg, and Otto Kirchheimer
    1939 *Punishment and Social Structure.* New York: Russell and Russell, 1968.
Sahlins, Marshall D.
    1958 *Social Stratification in Polynesia.* Seattle: University of Washington Press.
    1961 "The segmentary lineage: an organization of predatory expansion."
        American Anthropologist 63 (April):322–345.
    1963 "Poor man, rich man, big-man, chief: political types in Melanesia and
        Polynesia." *Comparative Studies in Society and History* 5 (April):285–303.
Sanders, William T.
    1968 "Hydraulic agriculture, economic symbiosis and the evolution of states
        in central Mexico." Pages 88–107 in *Anthropological Archeology in the
        Americas,* edited by Betty J. Meggars. Washington, D.C.: The An-
        thropological Society of Washington.
Sangar, Satya Prakash
    1967 *Crime and Punishment in Mughal India.* Delhi: Sterling Publishers.
Sansom, Basil
    1972 "When witches are not named." Pages 193–226 in *The Allocation of Respon-
        sibility,* edited by Max Gluckman. Manchester: Manchester University
        Press.
Savigny, Friedrich Karl von
    1814 *Of the Vocation of Our Age for Legislation and Jurisprudence.* London:
        Littlewood, 1831.
Schapera, Isaac
    1943 *Tribal Legislation among the Tswana of the Bechuanaland Protectorate: A
        Study in the Mechanism of Cultural Change.* London: Percy Lund, Hum-
        phries.
    1955 *A Handbook of Tswana Law and Custom.* London: Oxford University Press
        (second edition; first edition, 1938).
Scheff, Thomas J.
    1966 *Being Mentally Ill: A Sociological Theory.* Chicago: Aldine.
Schneider, David M.
    1957 "Political organization, supernatural sanctions and the punishment for
        incest on Yap." *American Anthropologist* 59 (October):791–800.
Schur, Edwin M.
    1971 *Labeling Deviant Behavior: Its Sociological Implications.* New York: Harper
        and Row.

Schwartz, Barry
1968 "The social psychology of privacy." *American Journal of Sociology* 73 (May):741–752.

Schwartz, Richard D.
1954 "Social factors in the development of legal control: a case study of two Israeli settlements." *Yale Law Journal* 63 (February):471–491.

Schwartz, Richard D., and James C. Miller
1964 "Legal evolution and societal complexity." *American Journal of Sociology* 70 (September):159–169.

Schwartz, Richard D., and Jerome K. Skolnick
1962 "Two studies of legal stigma." *Social Problems* 10 (Fall):133–142.

Scott, Robert A.
1976 "Deviance, sanctions, and social integration in small-scale societies." *Social Forces* 54 (March):604–620.

Scott, W. Richard
1964 "Theory of organizations." Pages 485–529 in *Handbook of Modern Sociology*, edited by Robert E.L. Faris. Chicago: Rand McNally.

Seidman, Robert B.
1969 "The Ghana prison system: an historical perspective." Pages 429–472 in *African Penal Systems*, edited by Alan Milner. New York: Frederick A. Praeger.

Selby, Henry A.
1974 *Zapotec Deviance: The Convergence of Folk and Modern Sociology*. Austin: University of Texas Press.

Selznick, Philip
1952 *The Organizational Weapon: A Study of Bolshevik Strategy and Tactics*. New York: McGraw-Hill.
1961 "Sociology and natural law." *Natural Law Forum* 6:84–108.
1963 "Legal institutions and social controls." *Vanderbilt Law Review* 17 (December):79–90.

Selznick, Philip (with the assistance of Philippe Nonet and Howard M. Vollmer)
1969 *Law, Society, and Industrial Justice*. New York: Russell Sage Foundation.

Service, Elman R.
1971 *Primitive Social Organization: An Evolutionary Perspective*. New York: Random House (second edition; first edition, 1962).

Shaw, Clifford R.
1930 *The Jack-Roller: A Delinquent Boy's Own Story*. Chicago: University of Chicago Press, 1966.

Shaw, Clifford R., and Henry D. McKay
1969 *Juvenile Delinquency and Urban Areas: A Study of Rates of Delinquency in Relation to Differential Characteristics of Local Communities in American Cities*. Chicago: University of Chicago Press (revised edition; first edition, 1942).

Shepardson, Mary
1965 "Problems of the Navajo tribal courts in transition." *Human Organization* 24 (Fall):250–253.

Shils, Edward A.
   1961   "Centre and periphery." Pages 117–130 in *The Logic of Personal Knowledge: Essays Presented to Michael Polanyi on His Seventieth Birthday, 11th March 1961.* Glencoe: Free Press.
Simmel, Georg
   1908a   "Conflict." Pages 11–123 in *Conflict and the Web of Group-Affiliations.* New York: Free Press, 1955.
   1908b   *The Sociology of Georg Simmel,* edited by Kurt H. Wolff. New York: Free Press, 1960.
Skolnick, Jerome H.
   1966   *Justice without Trial: Law Enforcement in Democratic Society.* New York: John Wiley.
Smigel, Erwin O.
   1956   "Public attitudes toward stealing as related to the size of the victim organization." *American Sociological Review* 21 (June):320–327.
Smith, M.G.
   1965   "The sociological framework of law." Pages 24–48 in *African Law: Adaptation and Development,* edited by Hilda Kuper and Leo Kuper. Berkeley: University of California Press.
   1966   "A structural approach to comparative politics." Pages 113–128 in *Varieties of Political Theory,* edited by David Easton. Englewood Cliffs: Prentice-Hall.
   1972   "The comparative study of complex societies." Pages 241–270 in *Corporations and Society.* London: Gerald Duckworth, 1974.
   1974   *Corporations and Society.* London: Gerald Duckworth.
Smith, Watson, and John M. Roberts
   1954   *Zuni Law: A Field of Values.* Cambridge: Papers of the Peabody Museum of American Archaeology and Ethnology, Harvard University, Volume 43, Number 1.
Sorokin, Pitirim A.
   1927   *Social Mobility.* New York: Harper and Brothers.
   1937   *Social and Cultural Dynamics.* New York: American Book Company.
Spencer, Herbert
   1876   *The Principles of Sociology.* London: Williams and Norgate. Volume 1.
Spitzer, Steven
   1975   "Punishment and social organization: a study of Durkheim's theory of penal evolution." *Law and Society Review* 9 (Summer):613–635.
Spradley, James P.
   1970   *You Owe Yourself a Drunk: An Ethnography of Urban Nomads.* Boston: Little, Brown.
Starr, June
   1974   "Turkish village disputing." Unpublished paper, Department of Anthropology, State University of New York at Stony Brook.
Steele, Eric H.
   1975   "Fraud, dispute, and the consumer: responding to consumer complaints." *University of Pennsylvania Law Review* 123 (May):1107–1186.

Steffensmeier, Darrell J., and Robert M. Terry
  1973 "Deviance and respectability: an observational study of reactions to shoplifting." *Social Forces* 51 (June):417–426.
Stephen, James Fitzjames
  1883 *A History of the Criminal Law of England.* London: Macmillan. Volume 1.
Stevenson, Robert F.
  1968 *Population and Political Systems in Tropical Africa.* New York: Columbia University Press.
Stinchcombe, Arthur L.
  1965 "Social structure and organizations." Pages 142–193 in *Handbook of Organizations,* edited by James G. March. Chicago: Rand McNally.
Sumner, William Graham
  1906 *Folkways: A Study of the Sociological Importance of Usages, Manners, Customs, Mores, and Morals.* New York: New American Library, 1960.
Sutherland, Edwin H.
  1929 "Crime and the conflict process." Pages 99–111 in *The Sutherland Papers,* edited by Albert K. Cohen, Alfred Lindesmith, and Karl Schuessler. Bloomington: Indiana University Press, 1956.
  1937 *The Professional Thief: By a Professional Thief.* Chicago: University of Chicago Press.
  1940 "White-collar criminality." *American Sociological Review* 5 (February):1–12.
  1945 "Is 'white collar crime' crime?" *American Sociological Review* 10 (April):132–139.
  1948 "Crime of corporations." Pages 78–96 in *The Sutherland Papers,* edited by Albert K. Cohen, Alfred Lindesmith, and Karl Schuessler. Bloomington: Indiana University Press, 1956.
Sutherland, Edwin H., and Donald R. Cressey
  1960 *Principles of Criminology.* Philadelphia: J. P. Lippincott (sixth edition; first edition, 1924).
Suttles, Gerald D.
  1968 *The Social Order of the Slum.* Chicago: University of Chicago Press.
Swanson, Guy E.
  1960 *The Birth of the Gods: The Origin of Primitive Beliefs.* Ann Arbor: University of Michigan Press.
  1967 *Religion and Regime: A Sociological Account of the Reformation.* Ann Arbor: University of Michigan Press.
  1971 "An organizational analysis of collectivities." *American Sociological Review* 36 (August):607–624.
Swartz, Marc J.
  1969 "Interpersonal tensions, modern conditions, and changes in the frequency of witchcraft/sorcery accusations." *African Urban Notes* 4 (February):25–33.
Sykes, Gresham M., and David Matza
  1957 "Techniques of neutralization: a theory of delinquency." *American Sociological Review* 22 (December):664–670.

Tannenbaum, Frank
1938 *Crime and the Community.* Boston: Ginn and Company.
Tanner, R.E.S.
1966 "The selective use of legal systems in East Africa." *East African Institute of Social Research Conference Papers:* Part E, Number 393.
Terry, Robert M.
1967 "The screening of juvenile offenders." *Journal of Criminal Law, Criminology and Police Science* 58 (June):173–181.
Thomas, Keith
1970 "The relevance of social anthropology to the historical study of English witchcraft." Pages 47–79 in *Witchcraft Confessions and Accusations,* edited by Mary Douglas. London: Tavistock Publications.
1971 *Religion and the Decline of Magic.* New York: Charles Scribner's Sons.
Thompson, Hunter S.
1967 *Hell's Angels: A Strange and Terrible Saga.* New York: Random House.
Thrasher, Frederic M.
1927 *The Gang: A Study of 1,313 Gangs in Chicago.* Chicago: University of Chicago Press, 1963 (abridged edition).
Tocqueville, Alexis de
1835 *Democracy in America.* Garden City: Anchor Books, 1969. Volume 1.
1840 *Democracy in America.* Garden City: Anchor Books, 1969. Volume 2.
1856 *The Old Regime and the French Revolution.* Garden City: Anchor Books, 1955.
Tönnies, Ferdinand
1887 *Community and Society.* New York: Harper and Row, 1963.
Turk, Austin T.
1969 *Criminality and Legal Order.* Chicago: Rand-McNally.
Turnbull, Colin M.
1961 *The Forest People.* New York: Simon and Schuster.
Udy, Stanley H., Jr.
1959 *Organization of Work: A Comparative Analysis of Production among Nonindustrial Peoples.* New Haven: Human Relations Area Files Press.
1965 "The comparative analysis of organizations." Pages 678–709 in *Handbook of Organizations,* edited by James G. March. Chicago: Rand McNally.
United States Federal Bureau of Investigation
1974 *Uniform Crime Reports for the United States: 1973.* Washington, D.C.: U.S. Government Printing Office.
van der Sprenkel, Sybille
1962 *Legal Institutions in Manchu China: A Sociological Analysis.* New York: Humanities Press, 1966.
van Velsen, J.
1969 "Procedural informality, reconciliation, and false comparisons." Pages 137–152 in *Ideas and Procedures in African Customary Law,* edited by Max Gluckman. London: Oxford University Press.
Wagner, Gunther
1940 "The political organization of the Bantu of Kavirondo." Pages 197–236 in *African Political Systems,* edited by M. Fortes and E.E. Evans-Pritchard. London: Oxford University Press.

Wallas, Graham
1914   *The Great Society: A Psychological Analysis.* New York: Macmillan.
Wanner, Craig
1974   "The public ordering of private relations. Part one: initiating civil cases in urban trial courts." *Law and Society Review* 8 (Spring):421–440.
1975   "The public ordering of private relations. Part two: winning civil court cases." *Law and Society Review* 9 (Winter):293–306.
Weber, Max
1904– *The Protestant Ethic and the Spirit of Capitalism.* New York: Charles
1905   Scribner's Sons, 1958.
1922a "Bureaucracy." Pages 196–244 in *From Max Weber: Essays in Sociology,* edited by Hans Gerth and C. Wright Mills. New York: Oxford University Press, 1958.
1922b *The Theory of Social and Economic Organization,* edited by Talcott Parsons. New York: Free Press, 1964.
1925   *Max Weber on Law in Economy and Society,* edited by Max Rheinstein. Cambridge: Harvard University Press, 1954 (second edition; first edition, 1922).
Welsh, David
1969   "Capital punishment in South Africa." Pages 395–427 in *African Penal Systems,* edited by Alan Milner. New York: Frederick A. Praeger.
Werthman, Carl, and Irving Piliavin
1967   "Gang members and the police." Pages 56–98 in *The Police: Six Sociological Essays,* edited by David J. Bordua. New York: John Wiley.
Westermeyer, Joseph J.
1971   "Traditional and constitutional law: a study of change in Laos." *Asian Survey* 11 (June):562–569.
1973a "Assassination and conflict resolution in Laos." *American Anthropologist* 75 (February):123–131.
1973b "Assassination in Laos: its psychosocial dimensions." *Archives of General Psychiatry* 28 (May):740–743.
Westley, William A.
1953   "Violence and the police." *American Journal of Sociology* 59 (August):34–41.
Wheeler, Stanton (editor)
1969   *On Record: Files and Dossiers in American Life.* New York: Russell Sage Foundation.
White, Leslie A.
1949   *The Science of Culture: A Study of Man and Civilization.* New York: Farrar, Straus.
1975   *The Concept of Cultural Systems: A Key to Understanding Tribes and Nations.* New York: Columbia University Press.
Whiting, Beatrice Blyth
1950   *Paiute Sorcery.* New York: Viking Fund Publications in Anthropology, Number 15.
Whyte, William Foote
1955   *Street Corner Society: The Social Structure of an Italian Slum.* Chicago: University of Chicago Press (second edition; first edition, 1943).

Wilson, Monica Hunter
    1951a *Good Company: A Study of Nyakyusa Age-Villages.* Boston: Beacon Press, 1963.
    1951b "Witch beliefs and social structure." *American Journal of Sociology* 56 (January):307–313.

Wilson, Richard R.
    1973 "Corporate organization and law." Unpublished paper, Department of Sociology, Yale University.

Winch, Peter
    1958 *The Idea of a Social Science and Its Relation to Philosophy.* London: Routledge and Kegan Paul.

Winter, Edward
    1958 "The aboriginal political structure of Bwamba." Pages 136–166 in *Tribes without Rulers: Studies in African Segmentary Systems,* edited by John Middleton and David Tait. New York: Humanities Press, 1970.

Wiseman, Jacqueline P.
    1970 *Stations of the Lost: The Treatment of Skid Row Alcoholics.* Englewood Cliffs: Prentice-Hall.

Wittfogel, Karl A.
    1957 *Oriental Despotism: A Comparative Study of Total Power.* New Haven: Yale University Press.

Yale Law Journal Editors
    1967 "Program budgeting for police departments." *Yale Law Journal* 76 (March):822–838.

Yngvesson, Barbara, and Patricia Hennessey
    1975 "Small claims, complex disputes: a review of the small claims literature." *Law and Society Review* 9 (Winter):219–274.

Zuckerman, Michael
    1970 *Peaceable Kingdoms: New England Towns in the Eighteenth Century.* New York: Random House.

AUTHOR INDEX

Numbers in italics indicate the pages on which the complete references are listed.

SUBJECT INDEX